# The Tele-Emergency Physician System as an Innovation in Prehospital Emergency Care

Rebekka Süss

# The Tele-Emergency Physician System as an Innovation in Prehospital Emergency Care

## An Economic Analysis Using the Example of the District of Western-Pomerania

Springer

Rebekka Süss
Greifswald, Germany

Submitted as a dissertation to the Faculty of Law and Political Science at the University of Greifswald.

ISBN 978-3-658-49560-2 ISBN 978-3-658-49561-9 (eBook)
https://doi.org/10.1007/978-3-658-49561-9

Translation from the German language edition: "Das Telenotarztsystem als Innovation der präklinischen Notfallversorgung" by Rebekka Süss, © Der/die Herausgeber bzw. der/die Autor(en), exklusiv lizenziert an Springer Fachmedien Wiesbaden GmbH, ein Teil von Springer Nature 2023. Published by Springer Fachmedien Wiesbaden. All Rights Reserved.

This book is a translation of the original German edition "Das Telenotarztsystem als Innovation der präklinischen Notfallversorgung" by Rebekka Süss, published by Springer Fachmedien Wiesbaden GmbH in 2023. The translation was done with the help of an artificial intelligence machine translation tool. A subsequent human revision was done primarily in terms of content, so that the book will read stylistically differently from a conventional translation. Springer Nature works continuously to further the development of tools for the production of books and on the related technologies to support the authors.



This Springer imprint is published by the registered company Springer Fachmedien Wiesbaden GmbH, part of Springer Nature.
The registered company address is: Abraham-Lincoln-Str. 46, 65189 Wiesbaden, Germany

# Foreword

Emergency care constitutes an essential component of the healthcare system, the significance of which is often underestimated. Since emergency care frequently involves urgent and life-threatening situations that permit neither delay nor any compromise in the quality of care, the appropriate planning, implementation, and monitoring of the necessary measures are of utmost importance for citizens and their life expectancy or quality of life. Within the relevant continuum of care, emergency medical services play a particularly important role, as they represent a highly sensitive phase in the process between initial care and acute hospital treatment.

The business administration literature has so far paid little attention to emergency care, and in particular to emergency medical services. Although there are individual studies on sub-disciplines (for example, air rescue), a systematic application of business administration concepts and tools to emergency medical services has scarcely taken place to date. This is all the more regrettable, as improvements in the efficiency of acute emergency care can directly lead to saving lives or enhancing quality of life.

This statement applies particularly to innovations in the rescue system, such as the tele-emergency physician system. This system was first developed and implemented in urban areas in Germany, while it was only the Land|Rettung project in the district of Vorpommern-Greifswald that enabled comprehensive coverage by a tele-emergency doctor. The project underwent a thorough medical evaluation, which alone would not have been sufficient to ensure its integration into standard care. For this, a health economic evaluation was indispensable.

This monograph by Rebekka Süss thus addresses a highly relevant and innovative topic. The author has undertaken the task of conducting a health economic analysis of the tele-emergency physician system in the district of

Vorpommern-Greifswald, thereby providing an economic evaluation of the tele-emergency doctor as an innovation in prehospital emergency care. In doing so, she makes an essential contribution to the further development of standard care in emergency medical services and, consequently, to acute medical emergency care in Germany. Above all, however, the health economic evaluation of the tele-emergency physician represents an independent contribution to the advancement of health management in a previously underexplored subfield.

In the Land|Rettung project, the author assumed responsibility for the design and implementation of the economic evaluation. This included designing the data collection process, recruiting partners for data collection, developing the relevant databases and additional instruments, data cleaning, data analysis, and evaluation. She arrives at findings of the highest relevance for academic healthcare management, thereby closing a research gap that has so far hindered further development of business administration applications in the field of emergency services. In particular, she succeeds in applying cost and queuing theory in this area. Furthermore, with this monograph, the author has made an important contribution to the fact that the tele-emergency doctor has now become part of standard care throughout Germany. It is extremely rare for dissertations to have an immediate practical impact on health policy. The author, in collaboration with the other project members of Land|Rettung, has achieved this.

Based on the high level of innovation and relevance of the topic, as well as the confident application of business management concepts in a highly significant yet often neglected sector of healthcare, I recommend this monograph to all readers who are willing to rethink healthcare and, in doing so, truly save lives.

Greifswald
in May 2023

Steffen Fleßa

# Gender Statement

To enhance the readability of the text, the masculine form is generally used to refer to persons, functions, etc. However, it is intended to represent all genders without exception.

# Contents

# List of Abbreviations

| | |
|---|---|
| BGB | Civil Code |
| FE | false call |
| ILS | Integrated Control Center |
| Max | Maximum |
| MD | Median |
| Min | Minimum |
| Min | Minutes |
| MIND | Minimum Emergency Physician Data Set |
| MV | Mecklenburg-Western Pomerania |
| MW | Mean |
| NEF | Emergency physician vehicle |
| RDPVO MV | Emergency Medical Services Planning Regulation Mecklenburg-Western Pomerania |
| RTW | Advanced life support ambulance |
| SD | Standard deviation |
| TNA | teleemergency doctor |
| UMG | University Medicine Greifswald |
| V-G | District of Vorpommern-Greifswald |

# List of Figures

# List of Tables

# 1 Introduction

Emergency rescue services in Germany have been following a strong trend for several years. The number of emergency service alerts is steadily increasing, particularly those involving emergency physicians. However, more and more often, there is no life-threatening situation for the patient at the scene.[1] As a consequence, the emergency physician is not always immediately available for life-threatening situations, as they may still be engaged in another mission. This results in long therapy-free intervals during which the patient does not yet receive medical assistance. Especially in rural areas, there are cases where an emergency physician must be dispatched from another, more distant location, further exacerbating the situation. In addition, there is a general shortage of personnel in the healthcare sector, particularly in rural regions. Prehospital emergency care is increasingly facing challenges in ensuring comprehensive, rapid, and high-quality patient care while complying with legal requirements. At the same time, there is cost pressure in the healthcare system and the need to ensure the financial viability of services.[2, 3] In 2018, healthcare expenditures in Germany amounted to 393,084 million euros, of which 5,340 million euros were attributable to emergency medical services alone. By 2020, these costs had already increased by 10% overall and by 18% in the area of emergency medical services.[4]

---

[1] See Marx et al. (2021), p. 138.

[2] See Brinkrolf et al. (2020), p. 7.

[3] See Fleßa (2014), p. 54 ff.

[4] See Statistisches Bundesamt (2022), online.



R. Süss, *The Tele-Emergency Physician System as an Innovation in Prehospital Emergency Care*, https://doi.org/10.1007/978-3-658-49561-9_1

Technological and medical progress, which continually leads to new innovations, is an important factor. Patient care also benefits from these developments, for example through digitalization. The situation in emergency rescue services is becoming increasingly acute, which is why, in recent years, many smaller, regionally tailored solutions have emerged in this field. These are often project-based and limited in duration, and are not always integrated into standard patient care. A potential way to supplement and support emergency rescue services is the teleemergency doctor system (TNA system). This has already been implemented on a project basis in several regions of Germany, such as North Rhine-Westphalia (since 2014 in Aachen)[5], Bavaria (since 2017 in Straubing), and Hesse (since 2019 in Gießen/Marburg)[6].

In Mecklenburg-Western Pomerania, a TNA system was introduced in 2017 as part of the Innovation Fund project of the Federal Joint Committee. The aim of the project was to expand and strengthen prehospital emergency care with the help of the TNA system (as one of four project measures). Existing resources are to be conserved and used efficiently.[7] The present dissertation forms the basis for the economic evaluation of the project and also discusses further aspects of this new form of care, as well as the advantages and disadvantages of various implementation options. The results of the study are intended to provide insight into the impact of deploying a teleemergency physician (TNA) on the deployment structure and the costs associated with a TNA system. Furthermore, the study examines to what extent the results can be transferred to other regions. Beyond the project, the individual solutions observed in many regions over the years raise the question of whether the establishment of a centralized TNA service is feasible. Therefore, the study also investigates whether centralization, compared to several decentralized TNA systems, can offer economic and other potential cost advantages.

To this end, Chapter 2 first provides a brief introduction to prehospital emergency care in general, followed by a focused overview for the district of Vorpommern-Greifswald (V-G). The Land|Rettung project, which forms the basis of this work, is also briefly presented. In this context, the teleemergency doctor system is introduced as a telemedical innovation, and implementation barriers to innovation adoption are highlighted. The fundamentals chapter concludes with an explanation of economic cost concepts and an introduction to the topic of queuing models.

---

[5] See Koncz et al. (2019), p. 683.

[6] See Humburg et al. (2021), p. 3.

[7] See Brinkrolf et al. (2020), p. 11.

Chapter 3 covers the methodology. It begins with a description of the Land|Rettung research project and the various data sets analyzed in the course of this work. These include the mission data from the V-G district for standard care as well as for the new form of care, the TNA system. In addition, the costs incurred and documented during the introduction of the TNA system are comprehensively analyzed. The chapter then provides a detailed overview of the data preparation and analysis of both data sets. Finally, the methodological approach used to transfer the TNA system to other regions is presented, along with the analysis of the feasibility and potential advantages of a centralized TNA service.

Following the structure of the work and the sequential research questions, Chapter 4 first presents the results of the analysis of the mission data. The evaluation is carried out according to various parameters (general trends, response times, participation rates of emergency physicians, TNA deployments, and mission durations), which are presented in sequence. Subsequently, the costs are broken down according to the cost items incurred, first in the project phase and then, based on this, under the assumption of standard care, divided into individual costs and average total costs. The standard cost function of a TNA system, derived from these results, is presented and explained in Sect. 4.2.3. In particular, the factors influencing costs are described. Section 4.3 concludes the results chapter by presenting the analysis results of a centralized TNA service compared to the decentralized alternative. Here, an operations research methodology is used to answer this research question.

The aim of the discussion is to critically examine the research hypotheses based on the results presented. This is carried out step by step, in line with the previous approach. First, the impact of the TNA system on mission development and system costs is discussed in Sects. 5.1 and 5.2. The transferability of the study results is then critically examined. Finally, the results of the centralization study are discussed, and the opportunities and risks of the TNA system are highlighted.

# Fundamentals 2

## 2.1 Cost Concepts

Internal accounting deals with management accounting, in particular cost and revenue accounting as well as planning accounting. It is primarily designed for internal company use[1] and is not subject to any legal regulations.[2] Cost and revenue accounting is divided into cost type accounting (What types of costs are incurred?), cost center accounting (Where are these costs incurred?), and cost unit accounting (For what purpose are these costs incurred?).[3]

First, the concept of cost will be briefly defined. According to Schmalenbach, costs are the "valued, performance-related consumption of factors."[4] In the broadest sense, costs can be described as the "valued use of factors, goods, or resources for the production of goods, services, or products."[5]

Cost type accounting, as the first component of cost accounting in general, aims to record all costs, classify them, and then systematically prepare them for further processing.[6] Depending on the objective of data preparation, various approaches to cost classification may be applied, and combinations of different criteria are also possible.[7] Table 2.1 presents the established bases for differentiation within cost type accounting.

---

[1] See Schweitzer und Baumeister (2015), p. 820.

[2] See Wöhe und Döring (2013), p. 642.

[3] See Eichhorn und Merk (2016), p. 310.

[4] Eichhorn und Merk (2016), p. 304.

[5] Eichhorn und Merk (2016), p. 305.

[6] See Schweitzer und Baumeister (2015), p. 936.

[7] See Plötner et al. (2010), p. 39.



R. Süss, *The Tele-Emergency Physician System as an Innovation in Prehospital Emergency Care*, https://doi.org/10.1007/978-3-658-49561-9_2

**Table 2.1** Cost types by basis of differentiation. (Source: Own illustration based on Wöhe (2013), p. 885)

| ***Basis of differentiation*** | ***Cost types*** |
|---|---|
| Type of consumed production factors | Personnel costs, capital costs, material costs, depreciation, … |
| Operational function | Procurement, storage, production, administration, and distribution costs |
| Capacity utilization | Fixed and variable costs |
| Time reference | Actual, normal, and planned costs |
| Type of allocation | Direct and overhead costs |
| Origin of cost goods | Primary and secondary costs |

The classification of costs according to input factors can include a wide range of cost types, such as *personnel, capital, material, or energy costs*.[8] This classification often forms the basis of cost type accounting.[9, 10]

When considering capacity utilization, a distinction is made between *fixed and variable costs*. Fixed costs arise from establishing operational readiness,[11] remain constant over periods, and are independent of the level of activity. In contrast, variable costs are characterized by their dependence on output volume. In addition to these two cost types, there are step-fixed costs, which remain constant within a certain output interval but increase abruptly when a threshold is exceeded, and then remain fixed again over the next interval.[12]

If costs are classified according to time reference, three cost types can be distinguished: *actual, normal, and planned costs*. Actual costs refer to the costs actually incurred during an accounting period, thus directly relating to the past. For normal costs, the actual costs of several periods are considered, resulting in an average cost value. If future costs are considered, these are planned costs.[13]

Another way to differentiate costs is by their attributability to cost units. Here, a distinction is made between *direct and overhead costs*. Direct costs (e.g., material

[8] See Eichhorn und Merk (2016), p. 311.

[9] See Wöhe und Döring (2013), p. 885.

[10] See Plötner et al. (2010), p. 39.

[11] See Wöhe und Döring (2013), p. 298 f.

[12] See Grünstäudl (2013), p. 24 f.

[13] See Grünstäudl (2013), p. 29 f.

costs) can be directly assigned to cost units. Overhead costs (e.g., rent) are allocated to individual cost units using a calculation rate.[14]

Finally, costs can also be differentiated according to the type of consumed cost goods. There are *primary costs*, where the consumed goods are procured externally, which applies to the majority of costs (e.g., personnel, interest, depreciation, and material costs). *Secondary costs*, on the other hand, arise from the provision of internal services.[15]

In practice, the classification by cost types usually follows classification recommendations developed for industry, resulting in company-specific solutions.[16] In principle, all costs incurred are collected within the framework of cost type accounting. The basis is the company's internal financial accounting, with the majority of costs generally classified as basic costs.[17]

The following section will provide detailed definitions of selected cost concepts that are relevant for the further course of this work.

"*Personnel costs* include all employee remuneration for the respective accounting period and thus reflect the monetary consumption of the production factor, human labor."[18] In addition to the so-called direct wage of the employee, which is reflected in the periodically incurred gross wage, there are also non-periodic personnel costs that must be taken into account. These include costs for vacation days, public holidays, continued payment of wages in case of illness, Christmas and holiday bonuses.[19]

In contrast to personnel costs, the term *material costs* can be defined. These refer to all other costs besides personnel costs. This classification of costs is frequently used in practice in the healthcare sector (e.g., in hospitals). When costs are classified into personnel and material costs, they are further differentiated by interest and similar expenses as well as taxes.

Assets are also considered material costs. The underlying useful life of the assets may differ from the legally prescribed period if this is necessary for a realistic representation of the circumstances. Furthermore, it must be defined which depreciation method is to be applied in this context. "*Depreciation* reflects the loss in value of assets. This may be caused by use (e.g., wear and tear), time (e.g.,

---

[14] See Eichhorn und Merk (2016), p. 317.

[15] See Wöhe und Döring (2013), p. 886.

[16] See Eichhorn und Merk (2016), p. 311.

[17] Weber und Schäffer (2014), p. 142.

[18] Schweitzer und Baumeister (2015), p. 938.

[19] See Wöhe und Döring (2013), p. 889.

**Fig. 2.1** Total cost function with fixed cost basis. *Source* Opresnik, Rennhak (2015), p. 165

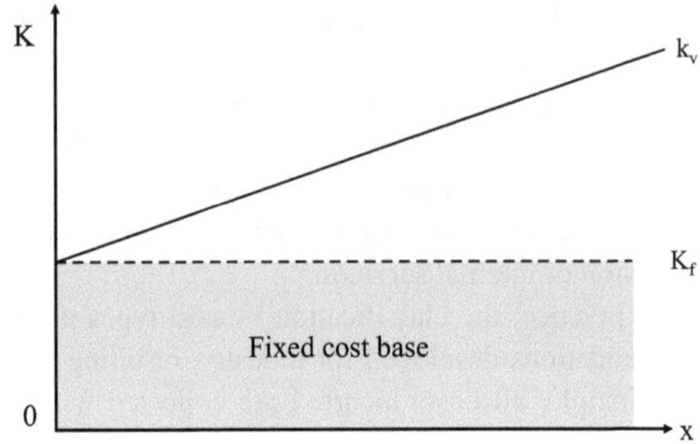


patent duration), or economic factors (e.g., bad debts)."[20] Straight-line depreciation, in which the same amount is written off each year, is frequently used in practice as it provides a steady cost level.[21] The annual depreciation amount is calculated by dividing the total depreciation by the useful life.[22]

If not only the individual cost types are considered separately, but the sum of the costs incurred during an accounting period, *total costs* are defined. These are typically composed of the sum of fixed and variable total costs per period. The respective cost types can be illustrated using graphs. Depending on the characteristics of the two cost types, different total cost curves may arise.[23] If fixed costs are present, this is referred to in the context of the total cost function as the so-called fixed cost basis.[24] *Average costs*, or unit costs, indicate the average cost per output quantity x. Since total costs are divided by the output quantity, both variable and fixed unit costs result.[25] If a linear total cost function is present, the course of the average cost function depends on the fixed costs. With constant fixed costs and increasing output, the fixed unit costs will continuously decrease, causing the unit cost function to decline. This process is referred to as fixed cost degression.[26]

Figure 2.1 shows the total cost function K, which consists of fixed costs $K_f$ and variable unit costs $k_v$ and depends on the output quantity x.

[20] Schweitzer und Baumeister (2015), p. 942.

[21] See Schweitzer und Baumeister (2015), p. 944.

[22] See Plötner et al. (2010), p. 51.

[23] See Grünstäudl (2013), p. 25 f.

[24] See Wöhe und Döring (2013), p. 299.

[25] See Wöhe und Döring (2013), p. 301.

[26] See Wöhe und Döring (2013), p. 301 f.

## 2.2 Prehospital Emergency Care

### 2.2.1 Overview

Emergency medicine aims to provide care to patients with severe illnesses or injuries as quickly as possible after the event occurs. There are various indications that necessitate emergency medical treatment. These can be described as follows

- (impending) impairment of vital functions (respiration, circulation, consciousness)
- (impending) damage to essential body parts or organ systems
- urgent and severe pain or agitation states[27]

In the event of an emergency, immediate action must be taken to save lives. The so-called rescue chain represents the components and sequence of the individual, consecutive steps of the emergency rescue services (see Fig. 2.2). According to Section 323c of the German Criminal Code, every citizen is obliged to provide assistance in an emergency situation, provided that there is no significant danger to themselves. The first task in the rescue chain is therefore the initiation of immediate measures by the first responder, such as securing the accident site. This must be followed as quickly as possible by an emergency call. The control center, contacted via 112, can, after assessing the background of the incident, dispatch the appropriate response unit. Until the rescue personnel arrive on site—which may take varying amounts of time depending on the location—first responders are required to begin first aid to the best of their ability. The control center serves as the interface between the first responder and the qualified emergency medical personnel.[28] The dispatchers at the control center decide, based on the situation described by the caller and the geographic location of the emergency, which response unit can be deployed.[29] With the alerting of the emergency vehicle or response unit, the on-duty paramedics or emergency physicians are informed that an emergency has occurred. They proceed to their response unit and travel to the scene.

[27] See Ziegenfuß (2021), p. 2 ff.

[28] See Kühn et al. (2010), p. 694 ff.

[29] See Justizministerium Mecklenburg-Vorpommern 08.10.2016.

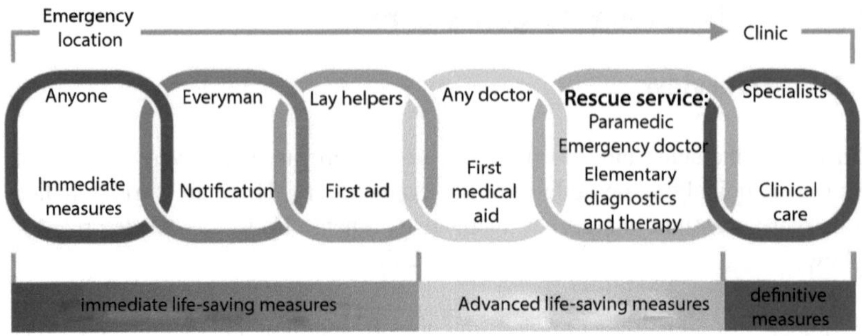


**Fig. 2.2** Rescue chain. *Source* Ziegenfuß (2021), p. 7

The control center performs several key functions within the emergency rescue services. These include, as previously described, the following activities:

- emergency call reception
- decision-making and alerting of the response unit
- coordination of emergency personnel
- incident documentation[30]

In addition to the well-known emergency number 112 for ambulance services, it is also possible to contact the on-call medical service via 116117. This service connects patients to local physicians if they are unable to visit a doctor and the situation is not acute. The emergency medical service, which is available nationwide during regular office closing hours, can be used for non-acute medical situations. However, the options provided by 116117 are apparently not sufficiently well known and are not widely used.[31]

Preclinical emergency care, along with patient transport, is one of the responsibilities of the public emergency medical services. It involves performing life-saving measures, ensuring the patient is fit for transport, and subsequently transporting the patient to an appropriate medical facility. The transport is carried out under the premise that no further harm is expected to result from the transport.[32]

---

[30] See Niehues (2012), p. 23.

[31] See Hahnenkamp et al. (2020), p. 255.

[32] See Hellmich (2010), p. 7.

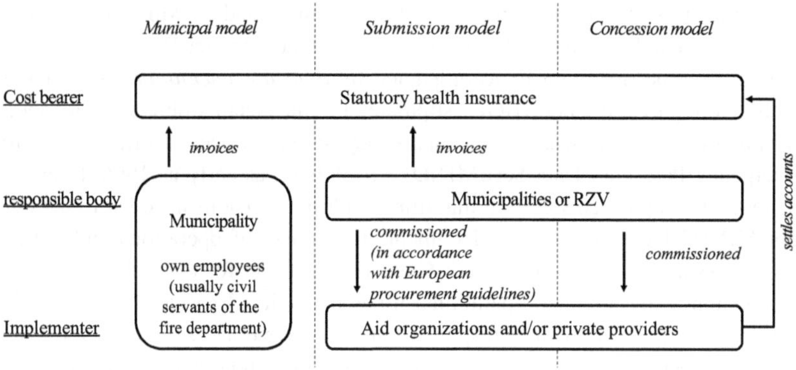


**Fig. 2.3** Organizational forms of emergency medical services. *Source* Deutscher Bundestag (2016), p. 9

According to Article 70, Paragraph 1 of the Basic Law, emergency medical services are organized and coordinated by the federal states, resulting in 16 different emergency medical service laws. The regulations vary significantly from state to state. The providers of ground-based emergency rescue services are the rural districts and independent cities, resulting in various smaller emergency service areas. There is also the possibility of forming an emergency service association, in which several districts or independent cities join together. Emergency medical services can be organized according to three different models: the municipal model, the concession model, and the tender model.[33] Figure 2.3 compares the three models and shows their cost bearers, providers, and operators. In the municipal model, emergency services are offered and organized by the municipality and billed to the health insurance funds. In the tender model, services are put out to tender to aid organizations or private providers by the public sector (e.g., municipality) in accordance with European procurement guidelines. In this model as well, the services are subsequently refinanced by the insurance providers. The last model, the so-called concession model, involves the municipalities selecting private providers or aid organizations through a transparent process and commissioning them to provide the services. In this case, billing is carried out directly by

[33] See Deutscher Bundestag (2016), p. 8 ff.

the service provider to the statutory health insurance funds.[34] Most German federal states, including Western Pomerania, use the tender model.[35]

Every rescue operation is accompanied by *data documentation.* Section 630 of the German Civil Code (BGB) stipulates the physician's obligation to document therapeutic treatment. For the emergency rescue services, the first Minimum Emergency Physician Data Set (MIND) was defined as early as 1996, based on the operational protocols used at that time. Multiple revisions have led to the current MIND3.1 data set, which documents the course of operations and patient care across a total of 14 modules.[36] These data include, for example, "structural data, technical rescue data, operational times [as well as] special features of the operation."[37] Each individual response unit must continuously report its status during an operation. This status provides information about whether and how the response unit is engaged, such as operational readiness at the station, en route to or departing from the scene, or the end of the operation. The rescue service personnel select one of the status codes 0 to 9 via a device in the emergency vehicle whenever the status changes. The status information is then entered into the computer-aided dispatch system, allowing dispatch center staff to take it into account for further operational planning.[38] In this way, the staff at the integrated control center (ILS) can determine from the status code whether a response unit that would normally be stationed near the scene is unavailable, and whether a response unit (with status 1 or 2) from a more distant station must be dispatched. An overview of the status messages can be found in Table 2.2. The status codes can only be reported in ascending order, although skipping numbers is possible. For example, there will be no status 8 for an ambulance (RTW) if the patient was not transported to a hospital.[39] Status 5 allows the crew to inform the dispatch center that an operation-related conversation is requested.

Rescue service deployment statistics have shown a trend in the dispatching of emergency physicians for years. The commitment of emergency physicians is steadily increasing, so that currently between 44% and 50% of emergency medical services deployments, in addition to the paramedic staff of the ambulance

---

[34] See Deutscher Bundestag (2016), p. 8 f.

[35] See Deutscher Bundestag (2016), p. 10.

[36] See Lohs et al. (2018), p. 392.

[37] Lohs et al. (2018), p. 392.

[38] See Hellmich (2010), p. 72.

[39] See o.V. (1999), p. 54 ff.

**Table 2.2** Status messages from response units to the dispatch center. (Source: Own illustration)[40]

| *Status code* | *Status message* |
|---|---|
| *0* | Emergency call |
| *1* | Available via radio |
| *2* | Available at station |
| *3* | Assignment accepted/en route to scene |
| *4* | Arrived at scene |
| *5* | Operation-related request to speak |
| *6* | Not available |
| *7* | Patient is being transported to destination |
| *8* | Arrived at destination |
| *9* | Manual confirmation/external registration |

(RTW), are accompanied by an emergency physician vehicle (NEF).[41] Not every deployment requires the presence of an emergency physician. The literature shows that only about 50% of cases actually require an emergency physician on site.[42] This situation leads to the resource of emergency physicians being increasingly tied up and unavailable for other cases. The rising number of emergency physician deployments also means that corresponding positions must be created and filled in order to meet the demands of emergency care.[43]

### 2.2.2 Response Unit and Personnel

In emergency rescue services, personnel are differentiated between *medical* and *non-medical staff*. The dispatch of the emergency physician is based on two types of deployment indications: either "patient condition-related indications," such as disturbances of consciousness and circulatory disorders, or certain standardized "emergency-related indications," such as fires, severe traffic accidents, or entrapments.[44] Due to their high level of qualification, emergency physicians possess full decision-making and operational authority and thus bear responsibility during

[40] See o.V. (1999), p. 54 ff.

[41] See Rossaint et al. (2017), p. 410.

[42] See Marx et al. (2021), p. 138.

[43] See Prasser et al. (2020), p. 151 ff.

[44] See Schneider et al. (2006), p. 54.

deployments.[45] The professional title of emergency physician requires additional training in emergency medicine, which primarily consists of various clinical specializations and a comprehensive emergency physician course.

There are various professional roles among non-medical emergency rescue personnel. Their training is diverse and differs particularly in scope. These include paramedics, emergency medical technicians, emergency medical assistants (until 2013), and emergency medical helpers. The following will focus on paramedics and emergency medical technicians. The specific training content also varies nationwide.[46] The aim of deploying an emergency medical technician is to initiate life-saving measures until the emergency physician arrives, thereby bridging the time gap. In addition, they ensure the patient is fit for transport and oversee the transfer to an appropriate hospital. Nationwide, it is common for the ambulance (RTW) to arrive at the scene before the emergency physician vehicle (NEF), so the RTW crew (e.g., including the emergency medical assistant) must initially rely on their own expertise. The time until the emergency physician arrives, which can be several minutes especially in rural areas (approx. 10–15 min), means that the emergency medical assistant is only authorized to perform a limited range of therapeutic interventions. This often leads to a tension in emergency care between the right to life and the right to physical integrity.[47]

There are various response units that can generally be deployed independently of one another. The medical personnel transported in the NEF are thus independent from the non-medical emergency personnel staffing the RTW. However, only the ambulance is equipped to transport patients, as it contains the necessary equipment for patient transport. In addition, there are response units such as rescue helicopters and patient transport ambulances, which, however, are not considered within the scope of this work.[48] A detailed description of the response units is provided in Sect. 1.2.2. Nationwide, approximately 3450 emergency ambulances are available for prehospital emergency rescue services around the clock. There are also vehicles that are used exclusively during the day and are therefore only staffed part-time.[49]

In Germany, the so-called *rendezvous system* has become established for emergency rescue services, meaning that the RTW and NEF response units are usually

---

[45] See Bundesärztekammer (2013), p. 3.

[46] See Eiff et al. (2016), p. 38.

[47] See Niehues (2012), p. 115 ff.

[48] See Brinkrolf et al. (2020), p. 2.

[49] See Niehues (2012), p. 124.

stationed independently of each other. Due to the higher number of RTW dispatches, the density of RTW stations is greater than that of NEF stations, as an emergency physician is not dispatched to every incident. In Germany, the RTW is always dispatched first. If the initial assessment by the ILS staff already indicates the need for medical intervention, an NEF is dispatched simultaneously.[50] During the course of an operation, ILS staff and on-site responders can request additional response units or stand them down if they are no longer needed.[51]

The following provides a brief overview of the individual emergency vehicles. Vehicles capable of transporting patients are also referred to as ambulances. Further distinctions can be made based on the type of deployment or transport, resulting in the designations RTW, general patient transport ambulance, and intensive care transport vehicle. The NEF serves as the emergency physician's transport to the scene. There are also rescue helicopters, which are likewise capable of transporting patients. All vehicles must be maintained at a current medical-technical standard.[52] However, since only RTW and NEF are relevant for the subsequent data analysis, further response units are not described in detail here.

The state rescue service laws additionally regulate the staffing of the RTW for each federal state. In Mecklenburg-Western Pomerania, an NEF is staffed by an emergency physician and an emergency medical assistant or paramedic.[53] Emergency physicians must, among other things, demonstrate additional qualifications in emergency medicine.[54] While an NEF is thus staffed by both medical and non-medical personnel, an RTW is staffed exclusively by non-medical personnel. The emergency physician is dispatched in cases where there is suspicion of impairment of vital functions, a defined indication, or when the patient is experiencing severe pain.[55]

An RTW, on the other hand, is staffed by at least one emergency medical technician and one emergency medical assistant. If no emergency physician is dispatched, the emergency medical technician can assist the emergency medical assistant in patient care. The vehicles are defined by requirements in the state rescue service laws and general DIN and EN standards. Of particular relevance is the European standard EN 1789 "Medical vehicles and their equipment—Ambulances," which

[50] See Hellmich (2010), p. 72.

[51] See Marx et al. (2021), p. 138.

[52] See § 3 RDG MV (2015).

[53] See § 4 RDG MV (2015).

[54] See § 4 Justizministerium Mecklenburg-Vorpommern 01.05.2015.

[55] See Hahnenkamp et al. (2020), p. 116.

defines the equipment and outfitting of emergency vehicles in detail. This standard has defined the requirements for response units nationwide since 1999. In principle, three categories can be distinguished, reflecting different levels of care. The first category includes types A1 and A2, which refer to patient transport ambulances. Type B defines the requirements for an emergency ambulance, and Type C those for a rescue ambulance. Patient transport ambulances of types A1 and A2 are used for general patient transport of individuals who are not classified as emergency patients. Type A1 is designed for the transport of a single patient, while a type A2 vehicle can transport multiple patients. Types B and C are used in the care of emergency patients.[56] According to EN 1789, a type B vehicle must be able to provide initial care at the scene, transport, and monitoring of the patient during transfer. Type C, in addition to the equipment of type B, is equipped with advanced medical-technical units (such as an advanced resuscitation unit).[57]

Nationwide, approximately 3,450 emergency ambulances are available for pre-hospital emergency rescue services around the clock. There are also vehicles that are used exclusively during the day and are therefore only staffed part-time.[58]

### 2.2.3 Financing

Emergency medical services are subject to dual financing, meaning that long-term investments can be supported by municipalities according to their financial capacity. The annual operating costs must be covered by the service providers themselves.[59]

The financing of patient transport services is regulated in Section 133 of Book V of the Social Code (SGB V). This states that "insofar as the fees for the use of emergency services and other patient transports are not set by state or municipal law, [...] the health insurance funds or their regional associations shall conclude contracts regarding the remuneration of services."[60] Section 70 SGB V further states that "the health insurance funds and service providers [...] must ensure a needs-based and uniform provision of care for the insured, in accordance with

[56] See Schmiedel et al. (2012), p. 42 ff.

[57] See Niehues (2012), p. 42.

[58] See Niehues (2012), p. 124.

[59] See Atzbach et al. (2016), p. 115 ff.

[60] Sozialgesetzbuch Fünftes Buch § 133 Abs. 1.

generally accepted medical knowledge."[61] It also states that "the care provided to the insured must be sufficient and appropriate, must not exceed what is necessary, and must be delivered in the required professional quality and in an economical manner."[62] Furthermore, the costs of emergency rescue services are not billed as medical health services under Section 27 SGB V. The health insurance only covers transport costs, as regulated under Section 60 SGB V, if there is a medical necessity for the transport.

The costs incurred in emergency medical services generally include fixed and variable costs. Fixed costs, such as for personnel and depreciation, account for up to 90% of the total costs in emergency medical services. These are incurred as so-called standby costs, as continuous operational readiness must be ensured.

### 2.2.4 Key Parameters

Within the scope of emergency rescue services, two types of missions for advanced life support ambulances (RTW) and emergency physician vehicles (NEF) can be categorized: primary and secondary missions. Primary missions constitute the actual spontaneous emergency rescue services and thus encompass a wide range of dispatch keywords. The patient to be treated has not yet been admitted to a medical facility prior to the mission. The primary mission is characterized by the rapid arrival of emergency personnel at the scene and prompt action. For 95% of emergency cases, a swift return transport to a hospital is not subsequently required. The type of rescue vehicle is irrelevant for the primary mission; it may involve air rescue or conventional ground-based rescue.[63]

Secondary missions, on the other hand, are planned operations. Examples include the transfer of a patient between two hospitals, transfer to rehabilitation facilities, or other medical institutions. Transporting a patient from their home to a medical facility is also considered a secondary mission.[64] Transport by ambulance can be carried out with or without emergency physician personnel. For the transfer of patients under intensive care, close medical monitoring during transport is required, for example.[65] If a patient must be transferred urgently or

[61] § 70 SGB V.

[62] § 70 SGB V.

[63] See Ahnefeld (1990), p. 362.

[64] See Kühn et al. (2010), p. 718 ff.

[65] See Hellmich (2010), p. 112 f.

in the event of a spontaneous emergency, the mission is classified as a primary mission. The observed reduction in the number of hospitals is increasingly leading to longer transport distances to transfer patients to an appropriate destination hospital. In recent years, the number of secondary missions has been particularly notable. In cases of medical necessity, this inevitably leads to increased demand for emergency physician resources. The shortage of medical personnel is in some cases already being addressed by deploying external emergency physicians.[66]

Within emergency rescue services, there are various parameters that are essential for patient care. The *response time limit* is an important parameter in emergency care. It is defined as the maximum time interval between the dispatch of the rescue vehicle and its arrival at the scene or the adjacent public road.[67] Regulations regarding the response time limit vary by federal state, usually concerning the specific time definition. Nationwide in Germany, response time limits range between 8 and 17 minutes.[68] If both ambulance and emergency physician vehicle are dispatched simultaneously, the ambulance usually arrives at the scene before the emergency physician vehicle.[69] The advanced life support ambulance crew can initiate first measures until the emergency physician arrives; however, due to their medical training, paramedics are legally limited in the scope of care they can provide.[70] Depending on the time of dispatch of the emergency physician vehicle, the time until the emergency physician arrives varies by federal state, reaching over 20 minutes for simultaneous dispatch and over 30 minutes if requested subsequently.[71]

Another important concept is the *therapy-free interval*, which describes the period from the emergency event to the initiation of specific therapeutic measures. In practice, this interval should be kept as short as possible to achieve the best possible medical outcome for the patient.[72] For certain indications, such as cardiac arrest, a prolonged therapy-free interval can lead to a poorer medical outcome.[73] The therapy-free interval is largely dependent on the response time limit.[74] If the advanced life support ambulance arrives before the emergency physician vehicle, this period must be bridged by the paramedics.

---

[66] See Reimann et al. (2004), p. 200.

[67] See Fleßa et al. (2016), p. 250.

[68] See Czaplik und Bergrath (2016), p. 319 ff.

[69] See Brokmann et al. (2015), p. 438 f.

[70] See Prasser et al. (2020), p. 151.

[71] See Czaplik und Bergrath (2016), p. 320 ff.

[72] See Seip et al. (2016), p. 99 f.

[73] See Rajan et al. (2016), p. 2095 f.

[74] See Hellmich (2010), p. 50.

In emergency medical services, there are recurring missions that are defined as *false calls*. Since pre-hospital emergency rescue services are defined by the transport of the patient to be cared for, emergency rescue services are not always provided for billing purposes by the health insurance. The reasons for a false call are varied. It may be that a patient is not found, refuses treatment in general, or is treated by the emergency services at the scene but not transported. Other potential reasons include cancellation of the mission due to weather conditions, cancellation of a resource due to lack of necessity, technical problems, the patient's death, or if the patient is not transported by the advanced life support ambulance.[75] In all these cases, a false call would be recorded in the computer-aided dispatch system at the end of the mission.

## 2.3 Emergency Rescue Services in Rural Areas

### 2.3.1 Definition and Challenges

There are various definitions of rural areas. In general, however, they are understood as exceptionally sparsely populated regions with significant distance from central cities.[76] The Federal Institute for Research on Building, Urban Affairs and Spatial Development particularly considers the proportion of settlement area and population density to delineate the concept of rural areas.[77] When examining rural regions, one must assume low population density and a low proportion of settlement area. A nationwide analysis of these characteristics reveals that, apart from the urban agglomerations around cities, many regions exhibit the features of rural areas.[78]

Many rural regions not only have low population density but also challenging landscape features such as coasts, lakes, or mountains. In addition, there are often difficult-to-navigate roads, bridges, or access routes, which can result in long response times for emergency services. These circumstances mean that compliance with the statutory response time limit is often not feasible in rural areas.[79] This particularly affects the time interval between the arrival of the ambulance

[75] See o.V. (2017), p. 1.

[76] See Schlömer und Spangenberg (2009), p. 17 ff.

[77] See Ried (2016), p. 2 ff.

[78] See Schlömer und Spangenberg (2009), p. 20.

[79] See Fleßa et al. (2016), p. 248 ff.

and the conventional emergency physician in rural regions.[80] Emergency care across state and especially national borders can pose further obstacles for emergency care and requires good organization and cooperation on all sides.[81]

Emergency medical care also faces a variety of challenges arising from the population structure. Demographic change is characterized by the migration of younger population groups to urban areas. Older people, who are often multimorbid or chronically ill, tend to remain in rural areas.[82] Increasing life expectancy due to medical and technological advances further leads to greater demand for health services. Urbanization in the health sector results in services being concentrated mainly in cities, leaving rural regions underserved.[83] Retirements in rural areas, combined with the migration of young doctors, result in relatively limited primary care options for patients, even as the demand for health services increases over time. In particular, this leads to a rise in the number of emergency rescue service deployments in rural regions.[84] Seasonal fluctuations in tourism also mean that, at times, emergency medical services must handle a disproportionately high number of emergencies. This requires not only resources in the form of advanced life support ambulances and emergency vehicles, but also the necessary personnel.

All these challenges in patient care are compounded by increasing cost pressures in the healthcare system due to rising healthcare expenditures.[85] There is thus a fundamental conflict between ensuring patient care and the efficient use of available material and human resources.[86]

Across Germany, there are a number of districts with a population density of less than 100 inhabitants per $km^2$ (see Fig. 2.4). In particular, the eastern part and the northern coastal regions of Germany have comparatively low population densities, with between 36 and 100 inhabitants per square kilometer.

If the topography of Germany is also taken into account, various landscape features become apparent. In addition to the coasts in the north along the Baltic and North Seas, there are numerous rivers, lakes, and mountains. These landscape features represent natural barriers that can pose challenges for local infrastructure and thus complicate patient care.

---

[80] See Skorning et al. (2011), p. 188.

[81] See Brinkrolf et al. (2020), p. 3 f.

[82] See Brinkrolf et al. (2020), p. 7.

[83] See Brinkrolf et al. (2020), p. 7.

[84] See Marx et al. (2021), p. 138.

[85] See Marx et al. (2021), p. 138.

[86] See Fleßa (2014), p. 54 ff.

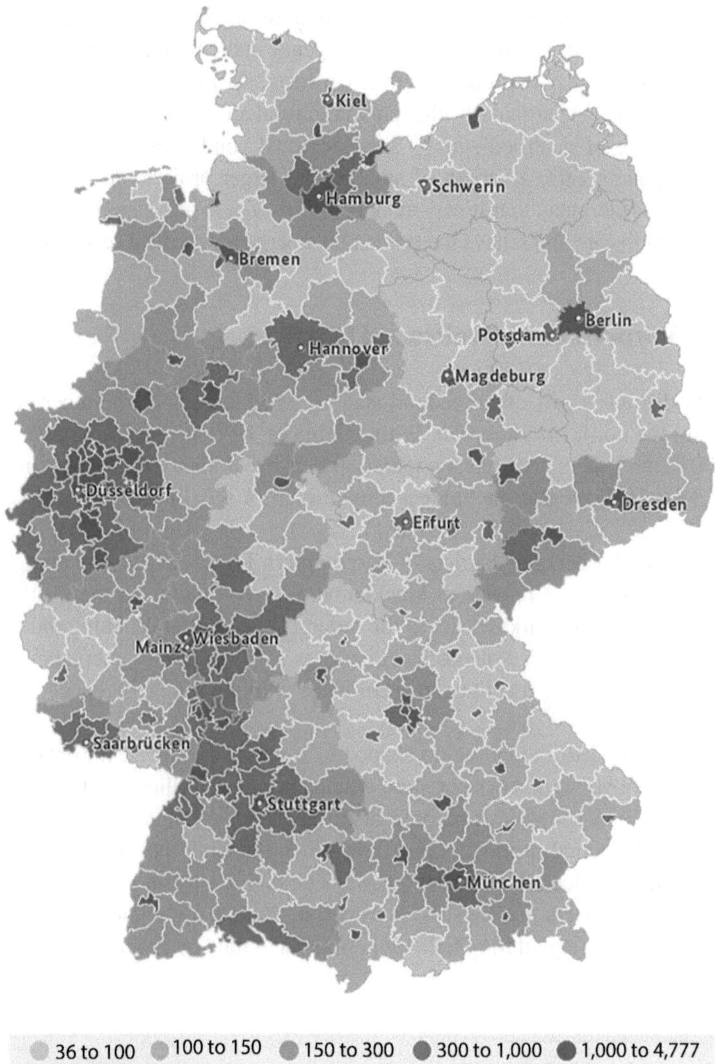


**Fig. 2.4** Population density in Germany 2019. *Source* Online[87]

[87] Online Bundesinstitut für Bevölkerungsforschung (2021).

To ensure long-term patient care, especially in rural regions, various approaches are being considered. Establishing new emergency stations (for emergency physicians and ambulances) could be effective. However, staffing these with emergency medical personnel is particularly challenging in rural areas due to the already widespread shortage of qualified staff.[88] Since regional conditions have a significant impact on patient care, a variety of smaller and larger projects are being implemented across Germany to test new models of care. These innovations are intended to close gaps in care and relieve the burden on emergency medical services.[89]

### 2.3.2 Vorpommern-Greifswald District

The V-G district is part of the federal state of Mecklenburg-Vorpommern and is located in the northeastern region. With an area of 3930 $km^2$ and a population of 236,000,[90] the V-G district has a population density of approximately 60 inhabitants per $km^2$. The region includes a long stretch of coastline with the Usedom peninsula.

The district borders the districts of Vorpommern-Rügen and Mecklenburgische Seenplatte, which also belong to Mecklenburg-Vorpommern. To the south, it is adjacent to the Uckermark district in the federal state of Brandenburg, and on the eastern side, V-G borders Poland. The district is responsible for emergency medical services and fulfills its duties in accordance with the state emergency medical services law.[91]

That the V-G district is a region shaped by tourism is evident, for example, in the number of overnight stays per year, which exceeds 5 million.[92] At peak times, up to one million people can be present in the district simultaneously, which is many times the actual resident population. When planning the structure of emergency medical services, such as the locations of stations, it is not only the regular provision for residents that must be considered. Particular attention must also be paid to peak loads (e.g., during holiday periods) and transport routes.[93]

---

[88] See Pfannstiel et al. (2017), p. 100.

[89] See Brinkrolf et al. (2020), p. 9.

[90] See Brinkrolf et al. (2020), p. 3 f.

[91] See § 7 RDG M-V (2015).

[92] See Brinkrolf et al. (2020), p. 4.

[93] See Hellmich (2010), p. 48.

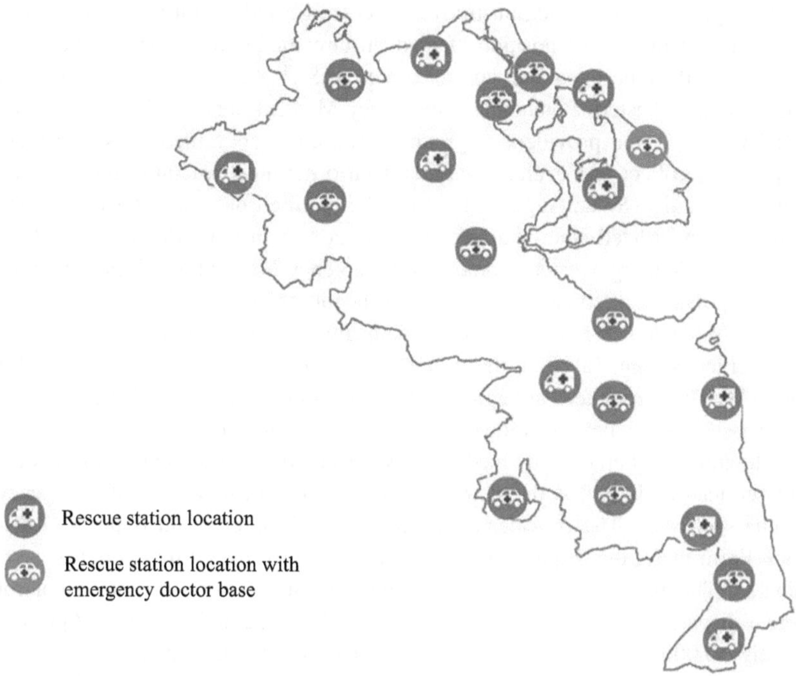


**Fig. 2.5** Emergency medical stations V-G (as of 2020). *Source* adapted from Brinkrolf et al. (2020)[94]

As shown in Fig. 2.5, there were a total of 20 emergency medical stations in the district in 2020, including 11 emergency physician stations. These stations provide a total of 27 ambulances (RTW) and 12 emergency physician vehicles (NEF) for the emergency care of the population. In response to recent changes in the care situation, the locations of the emergency stations have also been partially adjusted over time. Stations have been relocated, closed, or newly established in order to meet legal requirements for patient care, minimize response times, and thus optimize service delivery.

Emergency rescue services are managed and coordinated by the municipal emergency medical services enterprise, which is based in Greifswald. In addition

[94] Brinkrolf et al. (2020), p. 6.

to billing, accounting, administrative processing, and quality assurance, this entity also manages the position of medical director in emergency medical services as well as the integrated control center (ILS).[95] According to § 3 (2) of the Mecklenburg-Western Pomerania Emergency Medical Services Plan Regulation (RDPVO MV), the providers of ground-based emergency medical services are required to collect and evaluate various data to monitor structural, process, and outcome quality. Since August 31, 2018, the required data have been collected using a standardized state-wide electronic data system.[96] Furthermore, § 12 (2) of the Mecklenburg-Western Pomerania Emergency Medical Services Act (RDG MV) stipulates that so-called user fees are negotiated between service providers and health insurance funds. As a rule, the health insurance fund covers the costs of emergency care. In 2020, the user fee was €995 for an NEF and €1020 for an RTW. These user fees are agreed upon, for example, to cover depreciation of fixed assets, personnel operating costs, or non-productive trips.[97]

The municipal emergency medical services enterprise has commissioned various service providers[98] in the district to provide patient care as part of emergency rescue services.[99] The provider of the ILS based in Greifswald is the V-G district. From there, the dispatching of response units for the entire district is coordinated. The ILS employs a total of eight shift supervisors, seventeen control center dispatchers, and four staff members for IT and administration.[100] Approximately 50,000 emergency medical service deployments take place annually, of which 13,000 to 14,000 are carried out by the emergency physician.[101] During emergency calls, all mission-relevant information, actions, and time stamps are securely recorded by the ILS dispatchers. Through various interfaces, mission information is transmitted to other subsystems (telephone and radio networks, digital alerting network for all response units, geographic information system for resource locations).[102]

[95] See Brinkrolf et al. (2020), p. 6.

[96] See Justizministerium Mecklenburg-Vorpommern 08.10.2016.

[97] These values are taken from the document providing information on user fees in the public emergency services dated October 12, 2020.

[98] The service providers include: DRK Ostvorpommern-Greifswald, DRG Uecker-Randow, DRK Demmin, ASB Vorpommern-Greifswald, and HKS Greifswald.

[99] See Brinkrolf et al. (2020), p. 6.

[100] See Brinkrolf et al. (2020), p. 15.

[101] See Brinkrolf et al. (2020), p. 5.

[102] See Brinkrolf et al. (2020), p. 16.

The response time limit in Mecklenburg-Western Pomerania is defined in § 8 (2) No. 7 of the RDG MV. The response time limit describes the time from the alerting of the emergency vehicle to its arrival at a navigable road. Since the last legal amendment in 2015, it has been set at a maximum of 10 minutes for the first arriving response unit. In the case of an emergency physician alert, the response time limit for the NEF is 15 minutes. In addition, a safety level was introduced, stipulating that in rural areas (fewer than 20,000 inhabitants), 90% of response units must arrive at the scene within 15 minutes, and in urban areas (more than 20,000 inhabitants), 95% must do so.[103] Simulation calculations based on the district's mission data have shown that the required response time limit could not always be met. The analysis revealed that in six postal code areas, the response time limit for NEF was not met in more than 10% of cases. When examining the time interval from the arrival of the RTW to the arrival of the NEF, it became clear that in 14 of the 36 postal code areas, the interval exceeded five minutes.[104]

Studies also show that about 77% of the population in Mecklenburg-Western Pomerania can receive emergency physician care within 15 minutes. Approximately 70% receive professional medical assistance from advanced life support ambulance personnel (RTW) within the first 10 minutes. However, with regard to the therapy-free interval, this rate is considered critical.[105]

## 2.4 Telemedicine

### 2.4.1 Definition of Terms

For many years, medicine has had to respond to a wide range of developments and continuously adapt to meet changing circumstances. The challenges in rural areas described in Sect. 1.3.1, particularly demographic structural change, have an impact on the medical care of the population. Innovative concepts and structural adjustments in healthcare provision are necessary to ensure continued care for the population in the future.[106]

[103] See Brinkrolf et al. (2020), p. 6.

[104] See Fleßa et al. (2016), p. 250 f.

[105] See Seip et al. (2016), p. 100.

[106] See Braga (2018), p. 93 f.

According to the German Medical Association, the term telemedicine, as a subfield of e-health,[107] is "a collective term for various medical care concepts that share the fundamental approach of providing medical services in the areas of diagnostics, therapy, and rehabilitation, as well as medical decision support, to the population over spatial distance (or temporal offset)."[108] In this context, the use of information and communication technologies is of particular importance.[109]

The many and rapid developments in information and communication technology are also evident in medicine.[110] Telemedicine itself can be subdivided into several areas: teleconsultation, teletherapy, and telemonitoring. Teleconsultation includes, among other things, telemedical advice in acute situations, telemedical triage, and the transmission of other general medical information.[111] There are numerous ways to integrate or supplement telemedical innovations into healthcare provision for the population. Especially in rural regions with a shortage of skilled professionals, telemedicine offers great potential for patient care,[112] as medical staff do not need to be physically present on site, which, in addition to saving resources (medical personnel), also reduces the time required by eliminating travel distances.[113]

### 2.4.2 The Teleemergency Doctor System

#### 2.4.2.1 Project Land|Rettung

In December 2016, the Land|Rettung project, funded by the Innovation Fund of the Federal Joint Committee (G-BA), was launched in the district. The project ran for a period of over three years, from 15 December 2016 to 14 March 2020. The total funding amounted to 5.4 million euros. Through the GKV Health Care Strengthening Act (Statutory Health Insurance), the G-BA was commissioned to

---

[107] See Pfannstiel et al. (2017), p. 94.
[108] Bundesärztekammer (2015), p. 1 f.
[109] See Bundesärztekammer (2015), p. 1 f.
[110] See Kraft (2018), p. 702.
[111] See Braga (2018), p. 95.
[112] See Kuntosch et al. (2020), p. 136 f.
[113] See Braga (2018), p. 93 f.

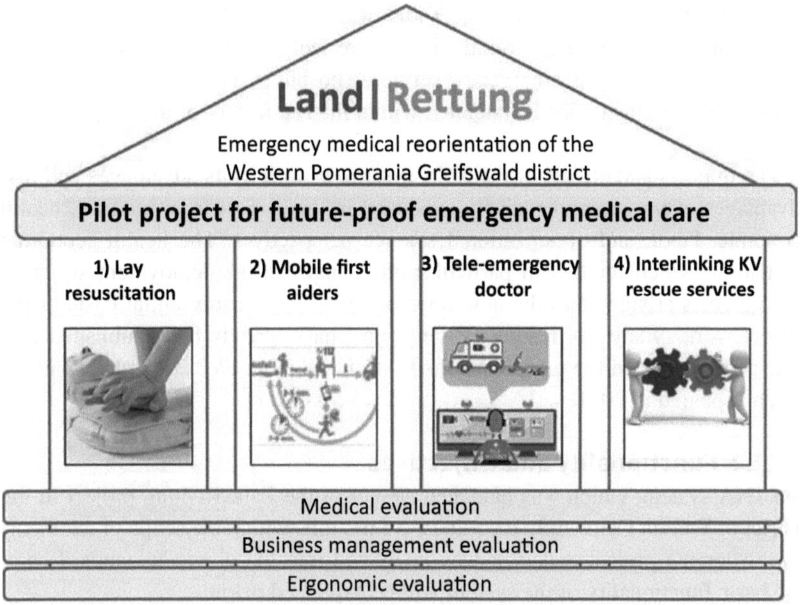


**Fig. 2.6** Concept of the LandlRettung project. *Source* Brinkrolf et al. (2020), p. 13

promote new forms of care that go beyond standard care and focus on cross-sectoral approaches.[114]

The barriers to emergency care in rural areas described in Sect. 1.3.1, particularly the challenge of bridging the therapy-free interval, were decisive for the orientation of the project. The project was based on four pillars aimed at improving emergency medical care in the model region of District V-G (see Fig. 2.6). In addition to strengthening resuscitation skills among laypeople, alerting first responders via app (mobile first aiders), and linking the collaboration between emergency services and the on-call medical service, a tele-emergency doctor system (TNA system) was also introduced.[115]

[114] See Brinkrolf et al. (2020), p. 14 f.

[115] See Brinkrolf et al. (2017), p. 142.

A distinctive feature of the project idea was, among other things, the interaction of various stakeholders from the healthcare sector (state government, district, health insurance funds, emergency services, hospitals, and the Association of Statutory Health Insurance Physicians) within the framework of the project measures.

The impacts and effects of the TNA system, as well as its advantages and disadvantages, were comprehensively evaluated in the project from medical, health economic, labor, and organizational science perspectives. The health economic evaluation, which focuses in particular on changes in the deployment structure and the costs arising from the new form of care, forms a substantial basis of the present work. Many key results of the project have already been published in a collected volume on the project results by Hahnenkamp, Fleßa, Hasebrook et al., which appeared in 2021.

### 2.4.2.2 Functionality and Objectives

The TNA system, which was launched as part of the Land|Rettung project in the district of V-G on October 4, 2017 at 7:30 a.m., falls within the scope of telemedicine. After the project ended, it was integrated into the district's standard care. The basic functionality of the system will be explained below.

The idea behind the system is that a telemedical emergency physician can be involved in an emergency at any time, so that medical expertise is available at the scene earlier.[116] Another objective of the TNA system is to use existing resources, especially emergency medical personnel, more efficiently[117] and to relieve the conventional emergency physician service, ultimately ensuring emergency medical care.[118] For this purpose, the tele-emergency doctor (TNA) was integrated into the rescue chain of prehospital emergency care (see Fig. 2.7). Like the response units RTW (non-physician personnel) and NEF (physician personnel), the tele-emergency physician is dispatched by the control center based on an indication catalog. Alternatively, the TNA can be contacted directly by the emergency medical personnel on site.[119]

This innovative form of care is part of telemedicine and is based on the use of modern information and communication technology. During their shift, the TNA

[116] See Brinkrolf et al. (2020), p. 12.

[117] See Schlechtriemen et al. (2007), p. 590.

[118] See Brokmann et al. (2015), p. 108 ff.

[119] See Gorgaß (2003), p. 560 ff.

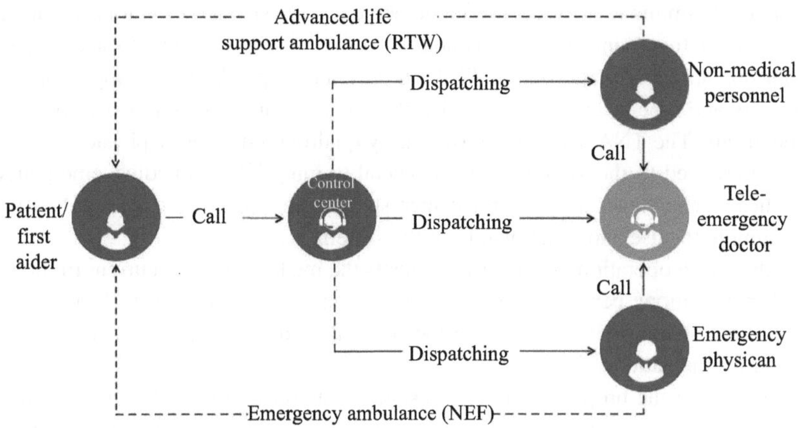


**Fig. 2.7** Rescue chain with TNA. *Source* Kuntosch et al. (2020), p. 119

is located in the so-called TNA center, from which they can participate in patient care provided by paramedics or emergency medical technicians over a spatial distance via audio and visual data transmission. For this purpose, the RTW is equipped with the necessary technology for the TNA service.[120] The central communication unit to the TNA workstation is a so-called peeqBOX, which is integrated into the TNA-RTW.[121]

The TNA workstation consists of several monitors on which the physician can view transmitted documents and the patient's medical parameters. Vital parameters (e.g., body temperature, weight, ECG) or photos can be sent to the tele-emergency physician in real time. In addition, the TNA can access Standard Operating Procedures (SOPs) and information on individual target hospitals during an operation, which provides valuable information for patient care.[122] Using the integrated video camera in the RTW, the TNA can also monitor the patient in real time and thus make well-founded decisions on medical interventions, which are then delegated to the emergency personnel at the scene.[123] It is possible to supervise several operations in parallel, but the data of different patients are never

---

[120] See Süss et al. (2020), p. 151.

[121] See Kuntosch et al. (2020), p. 131.

[122] See Kuntosch et al. (2020), p. 132.

[123] See Prasser et al. (2020), p. 151.

displayed simultaneously on the tele-emergency physician's monitors, reducing the risk of treatment and documentation errors.[124] The decision to accept parallel operations is made by the TNA on duty and depends, for example, on the severity and type of cases. Technically, there is no limit to the number of parallel operations. The TNA service is provided by qualified emergency physicians who are introduced to the system through special training.[125] Paramedics, emergency medical technicians, and control center staff must also receive comprehensive training in the use and functionality of the system.

During an operation, the TNA documents the medical history, current findings, and interventions performed in a protocol template, which is printed out at the end of the operation in the RTW for the hospital or, in the case of outpatient treatment, for the patient.[126]

As part of the project, a TNA workstation was set up in Greifswald, which is staffed year-round, 24 hours a day, seven days a week by a tele-emergency physician. In addition, telemedical equipment was installed in six RTWs. The locations of the TNA-RTWs can be found in Fig. 2.8 (two locations in Greifswald and one each in Wusterhusten, Loitz, Karlsburg, and Mellenthin).[127]

The TNA system offers several advantages. The therapy-free interval can be shortened, as the TNA can provide assistance as soon as the RTW arrives, without having to wait for the physical arrival of the emergency doctor. The TNA can also assist with diagnostics and delegation of therapy together with the emergency medical personnel en route to the hospital, so that the emergency doctor is not necessarily tied up and is available for further operations. In addition, the tele-emergency can support the on-site emergency physician with a second opinion.[128] Digital networking at the workstation also enables the TNA to consult guidelines in parallel with the operation. These options are not available to the conventional emergency physician during an operation.[129] Furthermore, travel times for medical assistance are eliminated, as the tele-emergency physician is only tied to the presence of an RTW supported by the TNA system, not to the NEF, unless only

---

[124] See Kuntosch et al. (2020), p. 133.

[125] See Süss et al. (2020), p. 164.

[126] See Kuntosch et al. (2020), p. 133.

[127] See Süss et al. (2020), p. 165.

[128] See Prasser et al. (2020), p. 152.

[129] See Brokmann et al. (2017), p. 110 ff.

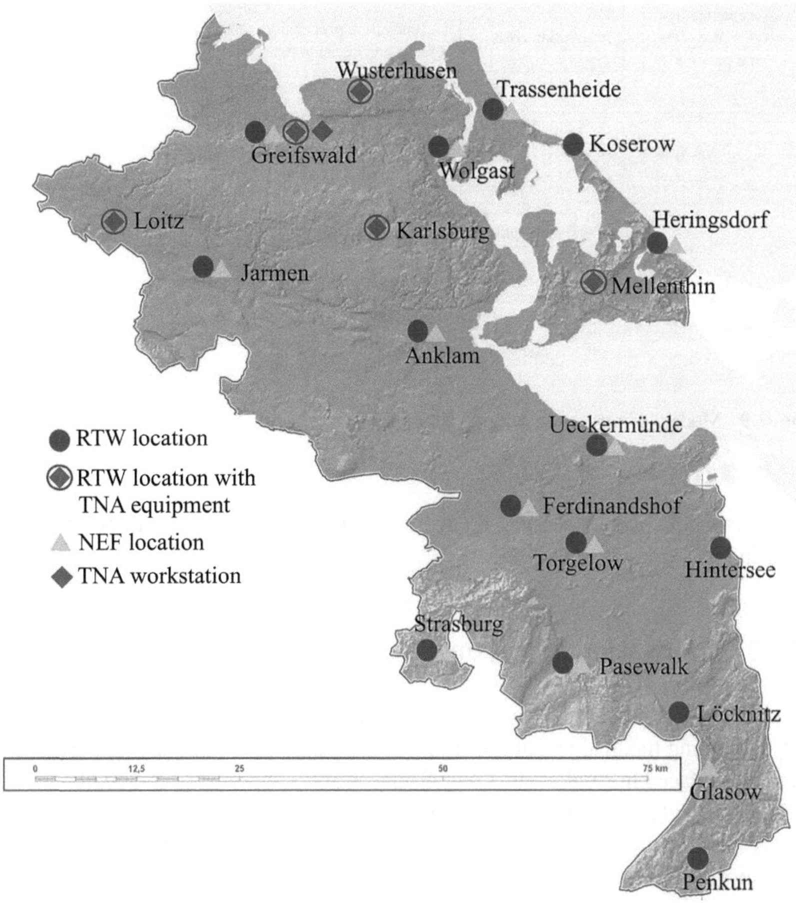


**Fig. 2.8** Rescue station and TNA locations in V-G. *Source* Süss et al. (2020), p. 165

audio communication is required. The factors described can promote the efficient use of the emergency doctorresource and lead to potential savings.[130]

The implementation of the TNA system requires numerous technical modifications, which are associated with various investments, for example in hardware

[130] See Kuntosch et al. (2020), p. 119.

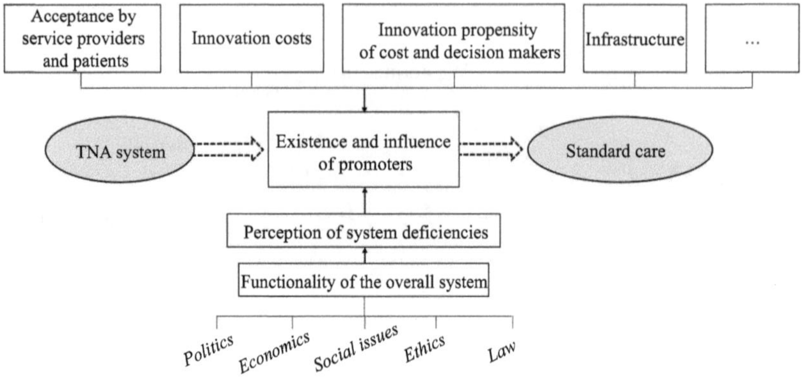


**Fig. 2.9** Model of innovation adoption for the TNA system. *Source* Süss, Fleßa (2020), p. 137

and personnel costs. A detailed breakdown of the costs incurred will be analyzed later in this work.

### 2.4.3 Innovation Adoption

The innovation potential in emergency medical services is high, as telemedicine, by decoupling medical assistance from location and action, directly addresses the challenges faced in rural areas. Long distances and a shortage of qualified personnel can be bridged through the use of telemedical applications.[131]

Despite the promising potential of telemedicine, the novelty of communication and information technologies creates implementation barriers. These are inherent to any new innovative technology, including the TNA system. Particularly in the potential transition to standard care, there are various influencing factors that can hinder the adoption of a telemedical innovation. Figure 2.9 provides a brief overview of the range of these different influencing factors.[132]

First, the technical infrastructure and the associated network coverage represent an important parameter. The TNA system is only effective if a connection between the ambulance crew and the tele-emergency physician can be established

[131] See Süss, Fleßa (2020), p. 136 f.

[132] See Süss, Fleßa (2020), p. 136 f.

at all times. Network expansion, especially in rural regions, is not always comprehensive or robust, which can lead to operational issues in the TNA system described.[133]

The acceptance of service providers is significantly dependent on the network infrastructure, as it is responsible for the smooth operation of the system. Recurring outages could negatively affect the acceptance of users and patients, as they may lead to dissatisfaction.[134]

The costs associated with introducing a new innovation must also remain in focus. These include not only investment costs but also annual operating costs incurred by new systems, all of which must be taken into account. Depending on the financing model for the innovation, costs can represent a major barrier to the adoption of an innovation. The costs of the TNA system, as an essential target variable of this study, will be analyzed and evaluated in the following sections.[135]

Finally, the role of promoters and their influence on the adoption of the innovation should not be overlooked. "Promoters are individuals who, based on their expertise, authority, or process knowledge, support the development, acceptance, and implementation of an innovation and help overcome implementation barriers related to lack of knowledge, willingness, or ability."[136] It requires individuals who are convinced of the innovation and are eager to share their enthusiasm with others. External conditions in politics, economics, society, ethics, and law must ultimately be continuously adapted to enable the adoption of the innovation.[137]

## 2.5 Queueing Models

A queueing model represents a situation involving the servicing of elements, resulting in the formation of a queue. Such model-based representations of real-world phenomena are found in many different areas of everyday life, for example in the service sector (e.g., doctor's office, supermarket checkout, etc.) or in road traffic (e.g., taxis).[138] Figure 2.10 shows an example of a queue with multiple service channels. The principle of the queueing model will be briefly explained using the example of a doctor's office.

[133] See Süss, Fleßa (2020), p. 136.

[134] See Rossaint et al. (2017), p. 411 ff.

[135] See Nolting und Zich (2017), p. 12 ff.

[136] Süss, Fleßa (2020), p. 137.

[137] See Süss, Fleßa (2020), p. 137.

[138] See Zimmermann (2008), p. 397.

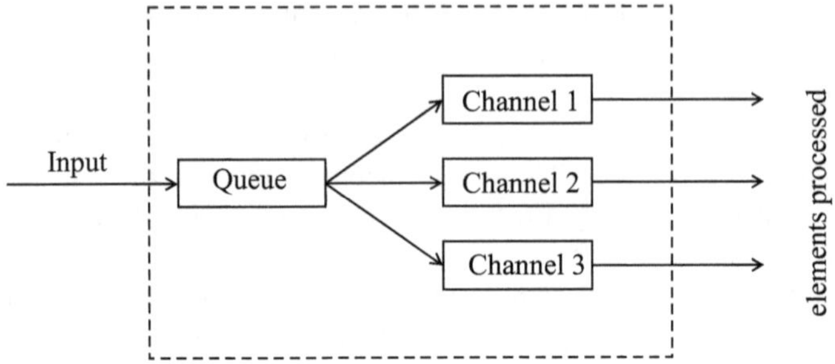


**Fig. 2.10** Queueing model with 3 channels. *Source* Zimmermann (2008), p. 399

First, there is an input, which, for example, represents an irregular and unpredictable flow of patients. Using one or more channels (the doctor as the service element), the patients are treated. Due to the continuous, usually irregular arrival of patients, a queue forms. The output of the model is the serviced patient, who leaves the practice at the end.

The model can be classified using Kendall's notation, which was developed by the British mathematician David George Kendall (*1918–†2007).[139] It consists of six symbols representing the different characteristics of the parameters. The general form is[140]

$$A|B|c|n|v|s$$

with

| | |
|---|---|
| A | Distribution of interarrival times |
| B | Distribution of service times |
| c | Number of service stations |
| n | System capacity |
| v | Number of possible customers |
| s | Queue discipline |

There are various parameters that are essential for describing and applying the appropriate queueing model. The arrival process describes how many elements

139 See Hedtstück (2013), p. 195.

140 Hedtstück (2013), p. 195.

arrive and at what intervals. The distribution and probabilities for the arrival of new elements must be defined *(distribution of interarrival times).* The servicing of elements in the queue should also be described as realistically as possible. In business administration, various processing methods are known that can describe different processes (e.g., FIFO—first in first out, or LIFO—last in first out)[141] *(queue discipline).* It is also possible that the capacity of the waiting area is limited, so that arriving customers must be turned away. Similarly, patients may be turned away if the queue or waiting time exceeds a certain threshold. Conversely, unlimited system capacity is also conceivable *(system capacity).* Furthermore, the servicing channels (e.g., doctors) must be classified. For example, is it possible for several elements (e.g., patients) to be serviced simultaneously by one or more channels *(number of service stations)*? Finally, a queueing model also requires information about the serviced elements and their probability of departure[142] *(distribution of service times).*

Depending on the characteristics of the parameters, the notation for each parameter is adjusted and the corresponding model is developed. The Poisson distribution is often used when the occurrence of an event is random and rare, and thus the probability of occurrence is very small. For Poisson-distributed events, the distribution of interarrival times is exponential with the density function $f(x) = \alpha e^{-\alpha x}$.[143, 144] These properties would be coded as an "M" in the first position of the notation (A). For unlimited system capacity (n) and number of customers (v), infinity is assumed and coded as "∞". It has become standard practice not to specify the last three positions of the notation if the default values $n = \infty$, $v = \infty$, and $s = \text{FIFO}$ apply.[145]

In order to use a queueing model to make statements about the probabilities of certain events occurring, the parameters of the model must be calculated. The average arrival rate λ indicates how many elements on average enter the system per unit of time.[146] The service rate μ indicates how many elements can be serviced on average per unit of time. It is calculated using the expected value for servicing an element.

[141] See Hedtstück (2013), p. 195.

[142] See Zimmermann (2008), p. 398 ff.

[143] See Zimmermann (2008), p. 403 ff.

[144] See Fleßa et al. (2021), p. 3.

[145] See Hedtstück (2013), p. 195 f.

[146] See Hedtstück (2013), p. 196.

# Methodology 3

## 3.1 Research Objective

This dissertation examines the deployment activities of the emergency medical services throughout the entire district of V-G. The impetus for this study is the tele-emergency doctor system, which was tested on a project basis starting in 2017. To assess the impact of this innovative form of care, two key areas were analyzed. First, the mission data of the district were analyzed using a pre-post comparison. Selected aspects of all mission data from ambulances and emergency physician vehicles prior to the system's introduction (2015 and 2016) were compared with the mission data from ambulances, emergency physician vehicles, and tele-emergency doctors from October 2017 to February 2020. Second, the costs associated with the implementation of such a system were also determined. The costs incurred as part of the Land|Rettung project served as the data basis. The municipal emergency medical services provided the cost information.

In addition to several targeted publications, the results of the Land|Rettung research project, which concluded in March 2020, were published at the end of 2020 in the collected volume "emergency care in rural areas" by Hahnenkamp et al. The results presented there already provide a general overview of the research work underlying this dissertation.



R. Süss, *The Tele-Emergency Physician System as an Innovation in Prehospital Emergency Care*, https://doi.org/10.1007/978-3-658-49561-9_3

## 3.2 Deployment Statistics

### 3.2.1 Datasets

The mission data of prehospital emergency care were provided by the municipal emergency medical services in Greifswald. The mission data from the entire district were continuously saved in the emergency medical services software for the response units ambulance and emergency physician vehicle. The software allowed filtering, analysis, or export of the datasets by column content (Fig. 3.1). Only economically relevant data such as mission number, response unit, date, time, location, and status update timestamps were used for analysis. Medical aspects and patient-related data were not exported from the software. The data for each observation period were exported into an Excel spreadsheet. The data from the pre-period (2015 and 2016) could be exported directly.

The mission data for the post-comparison period (October 2017 to March 2020) were continuously provided by the municipal emergency medical services after the end of each quarter for ongoing plausibility checks and data cleansing. The transmitted data sheet contained a total of 59 columns. Table 3.1 presents the most important column abbreviations and their contents.

The TNA mission data were provided by the service provider of the TNA system in an Excel spreadsheet. In addition, the mission data were digitally stored in the system and could thus be accessed in protocol form for each deployment via the provider's online tool. After each deployment, the on-duty tele-emergency physician also printed the corresponding incident report and filed it in a folder.

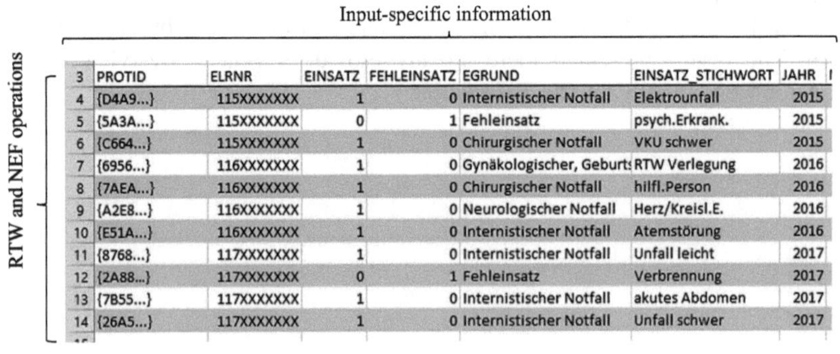


| 3 | PROTID | ELRNR | EINSATZ | FEHLEINSATZ | EGRUND | EINSATZ_STICHWORT | JAHR |
|---|---|---|---|---|---|---|---|
| 4 | {D4A9...} | 115XXXXXXX | 1 | 0 | Internistischer Notfall | Elektrounfall | 2015 |
| 5 | {5A3A...} | 115XXXXXXX | 0 | 1 | Fehleinsatz | psych.Erkrank. | 2015 |
| 6 | {C664...} | 115XXXXXXX | 1 | 0 | Chirurgischer Notfall | VKU schwer | 2015 |
| 7 | {6956...} | 116XXXXXXX | 1 | 0 | Gynäkologischer, Geburt: | RTW Verlegung | 2016 |
| 8 | {7AEA...} | 116XXXXXXX | 1 | 0 | Chirurgischer Notfall | hilfl.Person | 2016 |
| 9 | {A2E8...} | 116XXXXXXX | 1 | 0 | Neurologischer Notfall | Herz/Kreisl.E. | 2016 |
| 10 | {E51A...} | 116XXXXXXX | 1 | 0 | Internistischer Notfall | Atemstörung | 2016 |
| 11 | {8768...} | 117XXXXXXX | 1 | 0 | Internistischer Notfall | Unfall leicht | 2017 |
| 12 | {2A88...} | 117XXXXXXX | 0 | 1 | Fehleinsatz | Verbrennung | 2017 |
| 13 | {7B55...} | 117XXXXXXX | 1 | 0 | Internistischer Notfall | akutes Abdomen | 2017 |
| 14 | {26A5...} | 117XXXXXXX | 1 | 0 | Internistischer Notfall | Unfall schwer | 2017 |

**Fig. 3.1** Excel export from the emergency medical services software.

**Table 3.1** Dataset description emergency medical services software (RTW and NEF). *Source* Own representation[1]

| *Column abbreviation* | *Definition* |
|---|---|
| PROTID | Protocol identification number: alphanumeric code with specific patient reference |
| ELRNR | Mission number: mission-specific, multi-digit numeric code |
| FKENNER | Radio identifier: specific radio number of the emergency vehicle |
| EINSATZ | Binary coding for mission: true (1) or false (0) |
| FEHLEINSATZ | Binary coding for false call: true (1) or false (0) |
| EGRUND | Reason for dispatch: keyword-style cause of mission at mission start |
| EINSATZ_STICH-WORT | Dispatch keyword: keyword-style cause of mission at mission end |
| JAHR | Year of mission |
| MONAT | Month of mission |
| TAG | Day of mission |
| WOCHENTAG | Coding: Monday, Tuesday, Wednesday, …, Sunday |
| STUNDE | Hour of day at mission start |
| ANRUF | Time of emergency call received at the ILS [HH:MM:SS] |
| ALARM | Time of alerting the rescue station [HH:MM:SS] |
| AUSFAHRT | Time the emergency vehicle leaves the rescue station [HH:MM:SS] |
| ANKUNFT | Time the emergency vehicle arrives at the scene [HH:MM:SS] |
| ABFAHRT | Time the emergency vehicle departs from the scene (e.g., for hospital admission). [HH:MM:SS] |
| UEBERGABE | Time of patient handover, e.g., at the destination hospital [HH:MM:SS] |
| BEREIT | Time the emergency vehicle is available for the next mission (location unknown) [HH:MM:SS] |
| ENDE | Time of arrival at the station [HH:MM:SS] |
| HF | Response time limit: time interval from dispatch to arrival of the emergency vehicle at the scene |
| EORT, EORTPLZ and EORTORT | Location of incident: brief description of the scene, postal code, and name of the location |
| TORT, TORTPLZ and TORTORT | Transport destination: brief description of the destination, postal code, and name of the destination |

[1] See Schmiedel und Behrendt (2019), p. 14 ff.

Mission-specific information

TNA operations

| | Datum | E_Nr_BF | E_Nr_TNA | RTW | E_Art | Ei_Kat | E_Atyp | Kon_Be |
|---|---|---|---|---|---|---|---|---|
| 3 | Datum | E_Nr_BF | E_Nr_TNA | RTW | E_Art | Ei_Kat | E_Atyp | Kon_Be |
| 4 | 10.10.2017 19:34 | 117XXXXXXX | VG-20171010-10 | RTW04 | 1 | 1 | 1 | 10.10.2017 19:34 |
| 5 | 08.10.2017 10:43 | 117XXXXXXX | VG-20171008-5 | RTW14 | 1 | 1 | 1 | 08.10.2017 10:43 |
| 6 | 08.10.2017 17:59 | 117XXXXXXX | VG-20171008-7 | RTW02 | 1 | 1 | 1 | 08.10.2017 17:59 |
| 7 | 08.10.2017 20:15 | 117XXXXXXX | VG-20171008-8 | RTW02 | 1 | 1 | 4 | 08.10.2017 20:15 |
| 8 | 11.10.2017 03:34 | 117XXXXXXX | VG-20171011-2 | RTW05 | 1 | 1 | 5 | 11.10.2017 03:34 |
| 9 | 11.10.2017 10:56 | 117XXXXXXX | VG-20171011-9 | RTW15 | 1 | 1 | 1 | 11.10.2017 10:56 |
| 10 | 11.10.2017 20:43 | 117XXXXXXX | VG-20171011-13 | RTW02 | 1 | 9 | 2 | 11.10.2017 20:43 |
| 11 | 12.10.2017 14:54 | 117XXXXXXX | VG-20171012-5 | RTW11 | 1 | 1 | 1 | 12.10.2017 14:54 |
| 12 | 07.10.2017 09:37 | 117XXXXXXX | VG-20171007-2 | RTW05 | 1 | 1 | 1 | 07.10.2017 09:37 |

**Fig. 3.2** Excel export from the TNA data base software

Since all six advanced life support ambulances were equipped with tele-emergency physician technology over the course of several months, the first half-year after the system launch (from October 2017) is defined as the implementation phase. The data analysis, particularly with regard to the pre-post comparison, therefore includes the TNA mission data from the period 01.04.2018 to 28.02.2020.

The Excel spreadsheet of TNA missions comprised a total of 34 columns with information on the mission.

Figure 3.2 presents a sample excerpt from a data sheet from 2018. Here as well, each deployment is shown in a new row. No medical or patient-related data were available. The most important columns of the TNA Excel dataset are listed and defined in Table 3.2 below:

## 3.2.2 Data Preparation

### 3.2.2.1 NEF and RTW

The data sheet from the emergency medical services software comprised 59 columns. Some of these columns could not be included in the data analysis due to insufficient information and thus lack of comparability, so ultimately 27 columns were considered in the analyses.

The mission data reflected the deployment volume for the entire district during the respective observation period. Due to the large volume of deployment data, data cleaning was performed on a quarterly basis. Because of system interfaces, comprehensive plausibility checks of the mission data were of great importance. After an initial review of the mission data from 2015, a methodology for data cleaning and the associated plausibility checks was developed, which was applied

**Table 3.2** Dataset description (TNA deployments). *Source* Own representation

| *Column abbreviation* | *Definition* |
|---|---|
| Datum | Date of deployment |
| E_Nr_EB | Mission number as in emergency medical services software |
| E_Nr_TNA | Specific deployment number of a TNA deployment in the format<br>VG-YYYYMMDD-XY<br>(Coding: VG (district V-G), date (YYYYMMDD), and the current daily sequential number of the deployment (XY)) |
| RTW | advanced life support ambulance identifier |
| E_Art_korr or E_Art_Text | Numeric or textual information on deployment type (primary mission (=1), secondary mission (=2), or a consultation (=3)) |
| Kon_Be | Time of consultation start between TNA and RTW crew |
| Kon_En | Time of consultation end between TNA and RTW crew |
| Kon_Da | Duration of consultation between TNA and RTW crew |
| Gespr_Da | Cumulative duration of conversations between TNA and RTW crew |

to all datasets from the emergency medical services software. The aim was to check the plausibility of the mission data in relation to each other. The cleaning process comprised nine steps, which are explained in detail below.

***Step 1:*** *Check incident category*

In the first step, those deployments that were neither secondary nor primary missions were filtered out. Over the years, various other deployment types were documented in the columns EGRUND and E_STICHWORT, for example, transfer trips, refueling, washing, or deployments with the dispatch keyword "car repari shop".

***Step 2:*** *Adjustment and standardization of vehicle identifiers*

The designation of radio call numbers for RTW and NEF was adjusted independently of the project over the years of the observation period, resulting in different spellings of the call numbers in the datasets. In order to later perform an analysis by ambulance station, the spellings had to be compared, sorted, and standardized. The adjustment was made in the style of the currently valid call number ("3 letters for the station location", "differentiation RTW or NEF", "sequential number").

***Step 3:*** *Classification of emergency vehicles*

To analyze the primary and secondary deployment data of RTW and NEF, a new column "FART" was first added, which provided information on the vehicle type. Here, a distinction was made between RTW and NEF based on the call number. This additional filter option later simplified the analysis by vehicle type.

***Step 4:*** *Verification of protocol ID and deployment numbers*

The review of protocol ID numbers and deployment numbers revealed a large number of duplicates. Often, individual or multiple column values besides protocol ID and deployment number were identical. Solutions therefore had to be defined for different constellations. A brief case-by-case analysis showed that it is indeed possible for several people to be treated by a response unit during a deployment, but a number of 16 patients for one RTW is not plausible for capacity reasons (see Fig. 3.3). Due to the lack of patient-related information, it was therefore defined that only the assignment of a rescue resource is relevant for the analyses, not the number of persons treated. If all column entries of several datasets matched, this was defined as a duplicate. In these cases, all duplicate datasets were deleted so that only one dataset remained in the pool.

In cases where column entries differed and thus no obvious duplicates were present, the deployments were checked separately using the protocols in the

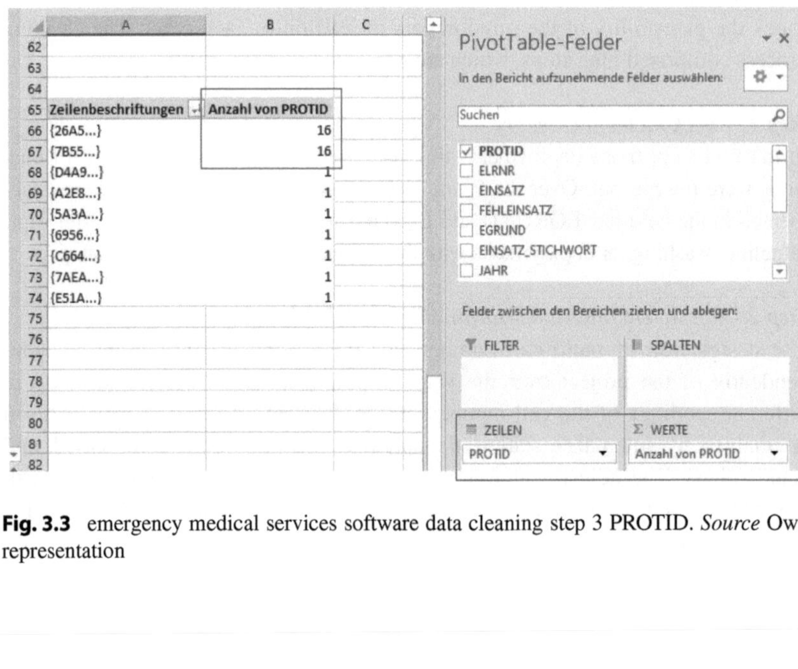


**Fig. 3.3** emergency medical services software data cleaning step 3 PROTID. *Source* Own representation

emergency medical services software to identify erroneous datasets. These may be due to subsequent changes in the incident report, which were later incorrectly imported as new deployments via system interfaces.

***Step 5:*** *Linking of mission data from RTW/NEF and TNA*
This step was only relevant for mission data after the introduction of the TNA system, and thus from the fourth quarter of 2017 onwards. From this point, in addition to the conventional RTW and NEF mission data, the second dataset with TNA data was also available. The linking of mission data from both systems was not automatic. In the dataset, the ILS only added the keyword "TNA" in the "EINSATZ_STICHWORT" column. Random checks showed that this information was not always valid, and the linking of the data had to be performed independently of this column.

The aim was to identify missions involving TNA participation in the emergency medical services software dataset using the new column "TNA Einsatz" ("yes" or blank). In cases where there was no TNA involvement, the column value remained blank. The basis for linking the data was the columns for mission number (column ELRNR) and vehicle identifier (column FKENNER), as these were the only two columns that uniquely identified a specific mission and were present in both datasets.

First, the order of the first five columns was adjusted so that mission numbers and vehicle identifiers appeared in the same columns in both spreadsheets. The TNA data from the observation period was then copied into the mission data of the emergency medical services software at the end of the table. Figure 3.4 illustrates the transition between the two datasets.

Next, the new column "TNA-Einsatz" was added to the table. The Excel concatenation formula was used to link the data.

"=VERKETTENE([@ELRNR], [@FKENNER])"

The result in each row was a seamless combination of mission number and RTW identifier, for example 17XXXXXXXRTW04 (see row 10). Using conditional formatting and the Excel function "highlight duplicate values," all concatenated entries that appeared at least twice were highlighted, making it possible to identify missions involving both a tele-emergency physician and an ambulance (RTW). The highlighted mission data were then filtered in the FART column for "RTW." For these RTW missions, "yes" was entered in the TNA-Einsatz column.

Before the telemedicine mission data could be deleted from the emergency medical services software spreadsheet (RTW and NEF), all filters were removed and the data was sorted again by any column. Since the row entries in the two

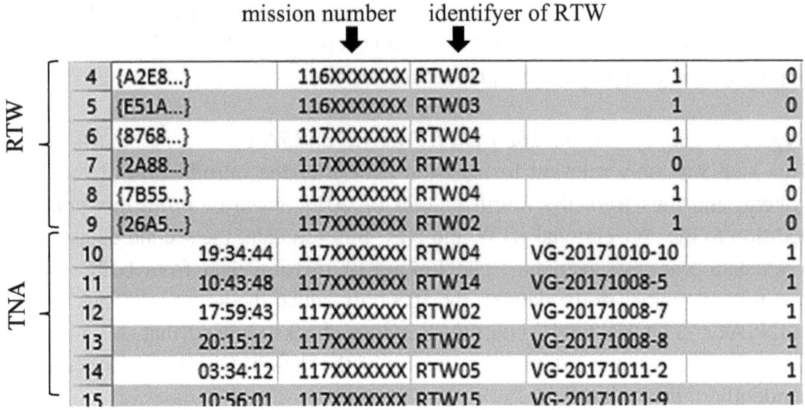


| | | | | | |
|---|---|---|---|---|---|
| 4 | {A2E8...} | 116XXXXXXX | RTW02 | 1 | 0 |
| 5 | {E51A...} | 116XXXXXXX | RTW03 | 1 | 0 |
| 6 | {8768...} | 117XXXXXXX | RTW04 | 1 | 0 |
| 7 | {2A88...} | 117XXXXXXX | RTW11 | 0 | 1 |
| 8 | {7B55...} | 117XXXXXXX | RTW04 | 1 | 0 |
| 9 | {26A5...} | 117XXXXXXX | RTW02 | 1 | 0 |
| 10 | 19:34:44 | 117XXXXXXX | RTW04 | VG-20171010-10 | 1 |
| 11 | 10:43:48 | 117XXXXXXX | RTW14 | VG-20171008-5 | 1 |
| 12 | 17:59:43 | 117XXXXXXX | RTW02 | VG-20171008-7 | 1 |
| 13 | 20:15:12 | 117XXXXXXX | RTW02 | VG-20171008-8 | 1 |
| 14 | 03:34:12 | 117XXXXXXX | RTW05 | VG-20171011-2 | 1 |
| 15 | 10:56:01 | 117XXXXXXX | RTW15 | VG-20171011-9 | 1 |

**Fig. 3.4** Illustration of the data merging process. *Source* Own illustration

datasets differed except for ELRNR and FKENNER, the TNA mission data were easy to locate, filtered, and then deleted.

***Step 6:*** *Check mission times*

The status times in the extract from the emergency medical services software were recorded in the format hh:mm:ss (hour:minute:second). Initial data analyses showed that not all time values for the various mission status messages were plausibly sequential. Even the auxiliary and mission times automatically stored in the emergency medical services software were sometimes implausible compared to the times of the various statuses. Therefore, the times from ALARM to END were checked step by step for plausibility.

Figure 3.5 provides an overview of the status verification process. For plausibility checking, temporary new columns were inserted to display the differences between the status times. Based on the sequence of mission status messages, each status was checked to determine whether the subsequent status was at least equal to the value of the preceding one. If this was the case, the value in one of the new "empty columns" was set to "TRUE"; if not, to "FALSE." To avoid incorrect results due to crossing the day boundary (midnight), the formula was constructed to calculate the time correctly (e.g., mission start at 23:49 and end at 0:16).

A column value already defined as "TRUE" in the first stage was included in the analyses. Since random samples showed that not all "FALSE" entries were actually implausible, two further verification stages were carried out. The results were filtered, and all "FALSE" fields were systematically checked again

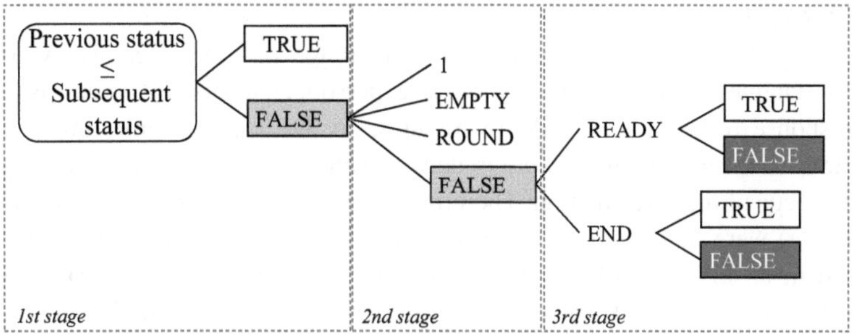


**Fig. 3.5** Status verification path in the emergency medical services software. *Source* Own illustration

in a second step. Cases in which individual times (presumably due to system interfaces) were rounded to whole minutes were adjusted. The plausibility of a time value compared to the other data for that mission was given, except for the aforementioned rounding, so these cases were labeled "ROUND" and included in the analysis. Another case involved missions where the subsequent time was always exactly one second earlier than the previous status ended. These cases were marked with "1." It was also assumed that these results were due to interface issues. These missions were also included in the evaluation and considered plausible. Missions for which individual column values did not contain time values (empty entries), resulting in an implausible mission sequence, could not be included.

If status entries remained defined as "FALSE" even after the second verification step, a third plausibility check was performed. For this, the columns BEREIT and ENDE were used. Both or at least one of these time entries must be reported by the ambulance crew at the end of each mission for the mission to be considered completed in the system and for the response unit to be available for a new alarm. If the immediate preceding status was empty, the last recorded status was identified and the time values were compared with those in the BEREIT and ENDE columns. Status messages without a timestamp can occur, for example, if no patient transport took place and thus the status TRANSPORT could not be assigned a time value.

A special case involved missions where, from a certain status onward, all subsequent status messages up to BEREIT or ENDE were empty. These missions could potentially be false alarms that were aborted from a certain status. If these missions could be verified as false alarms based on the false call column, they were included in the analyses.

***Step 7:** Check response time limits*

Reviewing the HF column revealed a wide range of time intervals. According to statements from emergency service personnel, plausibility decreases as the response time limit exceeds 35 minutes, so the response time limits were checked. The well-known software issue with handling day boundaries was a particular focus of the investigation. Therefore, missions that crossed a day boundary (midnight) were first filtered. For these cases, the response time limit was recalculated in an inserted column (time from alarm to arrival) and compared with the value given in the HF column. If the values did not match and the difference could not be explained by the rounding described in step six, the corrected value was adopted.

All response time limits were included in the analyses.

***Step 8:** Separation of primary and secondary datasets*

Finally, the primary and secondary mission data were separated. All missions containing an indication of patient transport or transfer in the EGRUND and/or E_STICHWORT columns were classified as secondary missions.

#### 3.2.2.2 Tele-Emergency Physician

It became apparent that there were discrepancies in the information recorded across the documentation channels of the TNA data. The time entries for the start of consultation ("Kon_Be"), end of consultation ("Kon_En"), and conversation duration ("Gespr_Da") stored in the various documents showed significant differences in some cases. This was likely facilitated by the system interfaces, resulting in not all timestamps being correctly transferred from the system to the present Excel table. In order to realistically capture and evaluate the time data relevant for the evaluation, a manual review of the mission data was conducted using the three documentation channels mentioned in Sect. 1.2.1: Excel spreadsheet, online protocol, and printed protocol. Due to the labor-intensive process of checking the time values and the late discovery of this issue, only data from the first quarter of 2019 onwards could be manually verified. For the mission data between 01.10.2017 and 31.12.2018, time discrepancies were estimated using statistical methods based on the verified data.

To provide an initial overview of the process of a telemedicine deployment and to illustrate the differences between the media, Figure 3.6 outlines the chronological sequence based on the deployment times defined in Table 3.2. The definitions of the time points and of consultation and conversation durations shown in the figure were confirmed by the service provider of the TNA system.

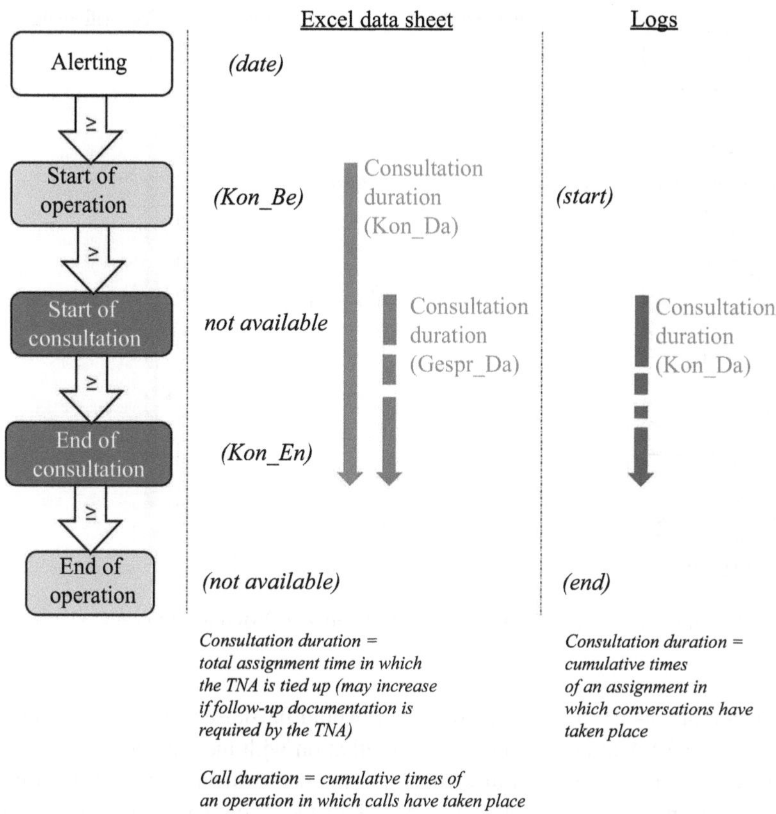


**Fig. 3.6** Overview of the chronological sequence of a TNA deployment. *Source* Own illustration

As shown in Fig. 3.6, there were differences in interpretation between the Excel spreadsheet and the protocols regarding the consultation duration and the times specified for the deployment. The information asymmetry between the Excel spreadsheet and the TNA protocols was used to achieve the best possible data collection for the upcoming analyses of deployment and engagement times of the tele-emergency physician. The reason for the differing interpretations of the values was not provided by the TNA system service provider. Therefore, the end of a deployment was recorded from the protocols in a correction column in

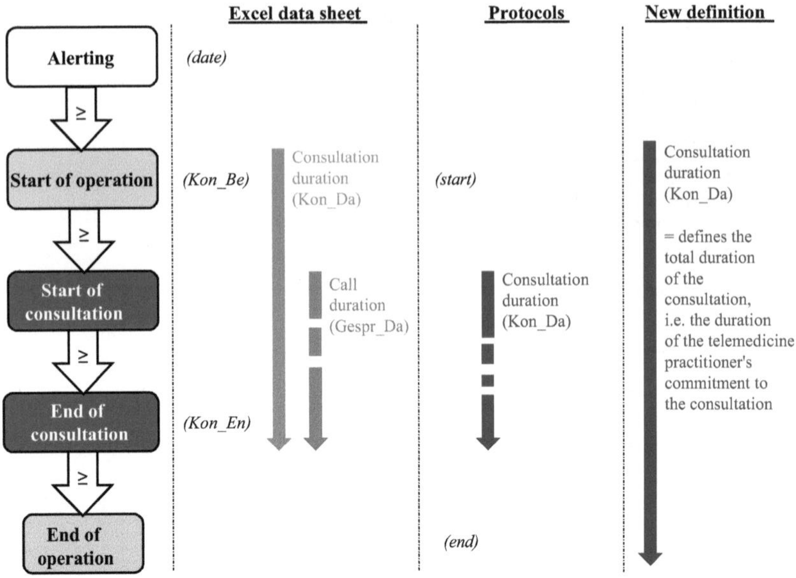


**Fig. 3.7** Adjusted data basis for TNA deployment. *Source* Own illustration

the data table, as it was assumed that there would be subsequent documentation work by the TNA after the end of the consultation with the emergency services. Furthermore, in the case of a discrepancy in the deployment start time, the time value from the TNA protocol was entered into the Excel spreadsheet in a new correction column. Figure 3.7 presents the final data basis for the analyses. It becomes clear that for the analyses, it was not the consultation end time available in the Excel spreadsheet, but rather the actual deployment end time that was relevant for assessing the engagement time of the tele-emergency physician. In most cases, there was a time gap between the end of the consultation and the end of the deployment.

After correcting the data for the start and end of consultations, the consultation duration was recalculated as the difference between the two corrected time points.

Since this information asymmetry was only discovered during the data cleaning for 2019, the data for 2018 had to be retrospectively corrected. A manual review of the individual deployment times was not possible due to time constraints. The following section describes the procedure for the retrospective data adjustments for 2018.

There were no clear correlations between the duration of deployment to be corrected and other deployment parameters. Therefore, for the mission data from the first to third quarters of 2019, the time differences between the originally recorded and the corrected consultation end times (time corrections) were first determined. Based on these calculated time values, a new sample for 2018 was generated using bootstrapping. For this, ten values were randomly and evenly drawn from the sample of time corrections (Q1/2019 to Q3/2019), and their mean (MW) was calculated. This mean then represented a new random value. This process was repeated as many times as needed for the number of adjustments required for 2018, so that each raw value could be assigned a random value from the same distribution as the corrected data. In this way, the erroneous times for deployments from 2018 could be adjusted, enabling an adequate analysis for the years 2018 to 2020.[2]

The differentiation of the TNA mission data was to be carried out using the "E_Art_Text" column. As already shown in Table 3.2, this column provides information on whether the case was a primary or secondary mission, or a consultation.

### 3.2.3 Data Analysis

Using a pre-post intervention comparison, the changes in the deployment structure in the V-G district resulting from the TNA system were to be illustrated. In analyzing the data, it was essential to distinguish between the number of data entries and the number of actual deployments (ELRNR), as more than one response unit was usually dispatched to a single deployment. In all analyses in this study, only the number of deployments is considered. Both deployments and false alarms were included in the analysis. Where necessary, these were reported separately, particularly for the analysis of temporal factors.

The entire observation period was divided into three sections. The pre-period extended from the first quarter of 2015 to the third quarter of 2017. Since the TNA system was introduced in the V-G district at the beginning of the fourth quarter of 2017, it was expected that the system would initially require some time to become established. For this reason, the period from the fourth quarter of 2017 to the end of the first quarter of 2018 was defined as a transition phase. The definition of this period was based on the experiences of the Land|Rettung project,

---

[2] Süss et al. (2020).

although a longer period could have been defined. However, since this period could not be included in the pre-post intervention comparison, as the total project duration was only three years, the duration of this transition phase was defined to be as short as possible and as long as necessary. From the second quarter of 2018 to the end of the data collection period on 29.02.2020, the post-period extended, representing the changes resulting from the introduction of the TNA system.

The mission data were analyzed with regard to four central areas: deployment trends, response times, participation rates, deployment times, and parallel deployments of the tele-emergency physician. In the pre-period, the mission data of the RTW and NEF were analyzed. In the post-period, the analysis of TNA deployments was added. In each analysis, primary and secondary deployments were evaluated separately. The following sections provide a content overview of the areas of analysis and describe the respective analytical approaches.

*Deployment trends over time*

The development of deployment numbers was intended to clarify how the incident statistics changed over the observation period. In particular, it was to be observed whether, after the introduction of the new system, a reduction in NEF deployments would be accompanied by a simultaneous increase in TNA deployments over time.

First, a basic analysis of deployment volume by vehicle type (RTW, NEF, and TNA) over time was conducted. For each criterion, the frequency of deployments was determined, differentiated by RTW/NEF and the tele-emergency physician.

Due to the telecommunication link between the tele-emergency physician (TNA) and the emergency medical service personnel, several aspects had to be considered when presenting the frequency of deployments. First, there were TNA deployments which, for example due to technical issues, did not have an incident number and therefore could not be linked to the ambulance (RTW) data. Thus, when determining the number of incident numbers (ELRNR) for the tele-emergency physician, it is necessary to also consider those deployments that do not have an incident number from the emergency medical services software. Furthermore, different TNA deployment numbers (E_Nr_TNA) may correspond to the same incident number from the emergency medical services software (ELRNR) if the tele-emergency physician contacted the advanced life support ambulance crew multiple times during a single deployment and the connection was interrupted in between. In the analysis of incident frequency, these deployments were therefore counted as a single unit involvement. The duration of TNA involvement in a deployment was also examined in detail at a later stage, with each connection between the TNA and the advanced life support ambulance crew being taken into account.

Next, the unit involvement of the stations was analyzed based on the total number of deployments. During the project period, only a few stations in the district were equipped with telemedicine-enabled ambulances. It was therefore necessary to examine whether the unit involvement of the vehicles at a station, or of the specific TNA-RTW, changed as a result of the introduction of the TNA system. For data protection reasons, the stations were numbered and not identified by location in the analyses. The same applies to the naming of the response unit. In order to compare the values from the pre- and post-periods, it is necessary to present the absolute number of deployments as average values, since the available pre-period covers four months more than the post-period. Therefore, the number of deployments is presented in the pre-post comparison using the average quarterly value for the observation periods.

The TNA-RTW were equipped as part of the project in the northern part of the district. However, staff at the southern stations were still able to consult the teleemergency physician by phone, but due to the lack of RTW upgrades, they could not use any additional communication units of the TNA system. It was to be examined whether the introduction of the TNA system led to a change in the incident frequency of the emergency physician vehicles (NEF) in the north compared to the south. The northern area included the stations in Loitz, Greifswald, Wusterhusen, Wolgast, Jarmen, Karlsburg, Anklam, Trassenheide, Zinnowitz, Koserow, Heringsdorf, and Mellenthin. Accordingly, Ueckermünde, Ferdinandshof, Torgelow, Strasburg, Pasewalk, Hintersee, Löcknitz, Glasow, and Penkun were assigned to the southern part of the V-G district. The analysis of incident frequency in the north-south comparison was carried out in accordance with the fundamental evaluation of deployment volume described in detail above.

In addition to the overall analysis of deployment numbers, a final analysis was conducted of the percentage of false alarms in the three observation intervals (pre, transition, post). For RTW and NEF, differentiation was made using the "Einsatz" column, as this indicated whether it was a deployment or a false call. For the TNA mission data, two columns were used to check for a false call. "E_Kat_Text" and "E_Atyp_Text" provided information on the category and type of deployment. If either of these columns contained a reference to a false call, the corresponding deployment was defined as a false call.

*Response Time Limits*

For the response time limit, only primary deployments were relevant, so secondary deployments were not further considered. The response time limit was evaluated at different levels for RTW and NEF. No response time analysis was conducted for the teleemergency physician, as it can be assumed that they became involved in the case shortly after the arrival of the participating RTW.

Initially, a pure pre-post comparison of the response time limit was conducted using the parameters mean, standard deviation, and median for each response unit. The mission data for the pre- and post-periods were each compiled in a table so that the analysis could be performed using a pivot table. For each response unit, the mean and standard deviation were first determined. The median was calculated using the following formula:

*=MEDIAN(IF(FKENNER=Y, response time limit column, "")*

Entries that did not belong to the specific response unit were not included in the calculation. This formula was applied for each FKENNER in the table of RTW and NEF deployments. In addition to the vehicle-specific analysis, the statistical parameters mentioned above were also determined for all mission data in the pre- and post-intervals.

*Deployment Times*

Using pivot tables, the number of deployments, the mean, and the standard deviation of the mission duration, as well as the median for all deployments of the response unit, were calculated for both the pre- and post-periods. The analyses were based on the columns mission duration and EINSATZZEITBEREICH from the emergency medical services software data. The data sets were analyzed separately for NEF and RTW. Analogous to the calculations for response time limits, the medians of the deployment times were also calculated using the following formula.

*=MEDIAN(IF(FKENNER=Y, mission duration column, ""))*

Furthermore, the distribution of incident frequency was determined according to deployment time ranges to show which deployment durations were particularly common in the data sets. The results are presented here using histograms.

The analysis of telemedicine deployment times was based on consultation and conversation durations. As already described in Sect. 3.2.2.2, consultation duration is defined as the period during which a teleemergency physician was involved in a deployment. The conversation duration, as the cumulative duration of actual conversations between TNA and RTW personnel, was also to be examined in order to illustrate the communication needs during the deployment. For the year 2018, the differences in consultation durations simulated by bootstrapping were used. From the first quarter of 2019 onwards, the times documented in the deployment logs, where available, were used for the analyses in the data set, and the consultation durations were recalculated accordingly.

Furthermore, ten time intervals were defined for the consultation time to facilitate the presentation of the number of deployments. These were five-minute intervals: less than 5 min, 6 to 10 min, 11 to 15 min, …, 81 to 85 min, and 86 to 90 min combined. In the last interval, all deployments in which the TNA was involved for more than 90 min (>90 min) were grouped together.

The evaluation of consultation and conversation times was carried out using bar charts, which in some cases were supplemented by frequency distributions. In addition, the statistical parameters mean, standard deviation, median, minimum, and maximum were calculated for the times.

*Involvement of NEF and TNA*

An important indicator of the functionality of the TNA system was the involvement rate of emergency physicians. Ideally, the emergency physician should not be completely replaced, but rather supported by the teleemergency physician.[3] The involvement rate reflected this. It indicates in how many cases an emergency physician or teleemergency doctor was present at the scene. Therefore, the involvement rate of the NEF was calculated from the pre- and post-data sets. For this purpose, a pivot table was used to determine in how many RTW deployments at least one NEF was involved. This number was divided by the total number of RTW cases in the observation period.

For the involvement of the teleemergency physician, which can only be evaluated in the post-period, a pivot table was used to determine, via the "TNA-Einsatz" column in the emergency medical services software data set, in how many RTW deployments a TNA was involved. This number was then divided, analogously to the calculation of the NEF involvement rate, by the total number of TNA-RTW deployments.

*Parallel Deployments of the TNA*

The use of tele- and video communication enables the tele-emergency physician to be involved in more than one case simultaneously. For example, during a transfer that does not require high-level acute medical intervention, the physician can also oversee additional cases. As already described in Sect. 2.4.2.2, the number of cases handled in parallel is not technically limited. However, the supervision of concurrent cases is always at the discretion of the on-duty tele-emergency physician and depends on the specific case context. To contextualize the results of

[3] See Süss et al. (2020), p. 167.

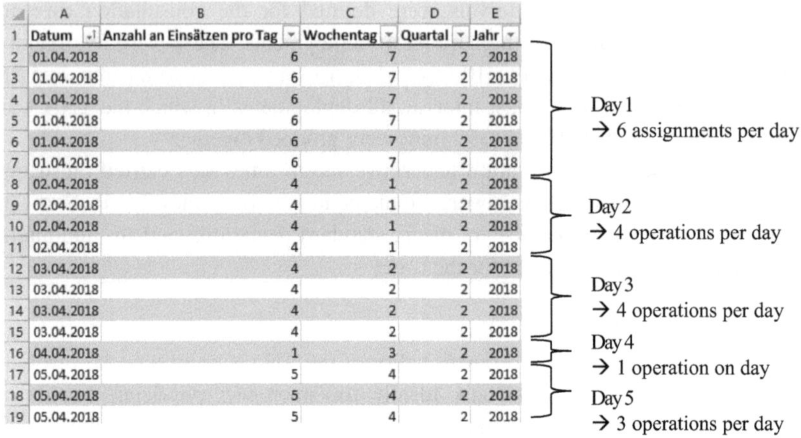

| | A | B | C | D | E |
|---|---|---|---|---|---|
| 1 | Datum | Anzahl an Einsätzen pro Tag | Wochentag | Quartal | Jahr |
| 2 | 01.04.2018 | 6 | 7 | 2 | 2018 |
| 3 | 01.04.2018 | 6 | 7 | 2 | 2018 |
| 4 | 01.04.2018 | 6 | 7 | 2 | 2018 |
| 5 | 01.04.2018 | 6 | 7 | 2 | 2018 |
| 6 | 01.04.2018 | 6 | 7 | 2 | 2018 |
| 7 | 01.04.2018 | 6 | 7 | 2 | 2018 |
| 8 | 02.04.2018 | 4 | 1 | 2 | 2018 |
| 9 | 02.04.2018 | 4 | 1 | 2 | 2018 |
| 10 | 02.04.2018 | 4 | 1 | 2 | 2018 |
| 11 | 02.04.2018 | 4 | 1 | 2 | 2018 |
| 12 | 03.04.2018 | 4 | 2 | 2 | 2018 |
| 13 | 03.04.2018 | 4 | 2 | 2 | 2018 |
| 14 | 03.04.2018 | 4 | 2 | 2 | 2018 |
| 15 | 03.04.2018 | 4 | 2 | 2 | 2018 |
| 16 | 04.04.2018 | 1 | 3 | 2 | 2018 |
| 17 | 05.04.2018 | 5 | 4 | 2 | 2018 |
| 18 | 05.04.2018 | 5 | 4 | 2 | 2018 |
| 19 | 05.04.2018 | 5 | 4 | 2 | 2018 |



**Fig. 3.8** Calculation of TNA cases per day. *Source* Own illustration

the analysis of parallel cases in the post-period, the telemedical cases were first descriptively analyzed by day, weekday, and time of day. The analyses were based on the telemedical mission data table.

The analysis by *day* was intended to show how many TNA cases occurred on a given day. For this purpose, a new column was first inserted. Using the "COUNTIF" function, the number of times the date of the respective case appeared in the data sheet was determined for each row based on the entries in the "Date" column (see Fig. 3.8). Subsequently, a pivot table was used to calculate how many row entries there were for each number of cases per day. In the final step, this sum had to be divided by the number of cases per day to determine the number of days with a specific number of cases per day. In addition to a graphical representation of the frequency distribution as a bar chart, the mean, minimum, and maximum number of cases per day were also calculated.

Furthermore, it was examined whether there was a concentration of cases on specific *weekdays*. For this purpose, all records from the post-period were considered simultaneously. Using a pivot table in Excel, the frequency of the numbers 1 to 7 in the "Weekday" column was counted. The numbers in the dataset were coded as follows: 1 = Monday, 2 = Tuesday, 3 = Wednesday, etc., up to 7 = Sunday. The total number of cases per weekday was compared, and the minimum and maximum were determined.

Before analyzing parallel cases during the observation period, an evaluation by *time of day* was conducted. The aim was to determine at which times TNA cases occurred most frequently. It was hypothesized that these times might be related to the times at which parallel cases occurred. To calculate the distribution of cases by time of day, the start of the consultation was used as the basis. For this, a new column was added to the data sheet, containing either the entry for the corrected consultation start (possible from 2019 onwards) or the originally recorded start of the consultation. Thus, each case could be assigned a consultation start time, provided an entry was available in one of the two columns. Next, five time-of-day categories were defined. The first time interval was aligned with the start of the 24-hour shift in the district, beginning at 08:00:00 and ending at 11:59:59, with all cases whose consultation started within this interval assigned accordingly. The next interval included all cases with a consultation start between 12:00:00 and 15:59:59, then 16:00:00 to 19:59:59, 20:00:00 to 23:59:59, 24:00:00 to 03:59:59, and finally 04:00:00 to 07:59:59.

Subsequently, the number of records for each time-of-day category was again counted using a pivot table. Additionally, the consultation time was set as a filter, and the number of cases in each time-of-day category was determined for each consultation duration category. To simplify the presentation of results, the originally ten consultation duration categories were consolidated into four new intervals (less than 15 min, 16 to 30 min, 31 to 45 min, and more than 45 min). In the final step, the proportions of cases per consultation duration and per time-of-day category were calculated relative to the total number of cases.

## 3.3 Cost Analysis

### 3.3.1 Data Basis

The data basis consisted of the costs incurred during the introduction of the TNA system in the V-G district. First, all costs incurred from October 2017 to December 2018 were compiled from the financial accounting of the emergency medical services municipal enterprise. These costs could be clearly separated from the costs of conventional standard care in the district (ground and air), as the TNA center was set up in a different location from the emergency physician center. In addition, during the project, regular emergency care was separated from the tele-emergency physician service not only legally but also in accounting terms. Since the description of individual cost items was not always self-explanatory, unclear cost items were discussed in detail with the staff of the emergency medical services municipal enterprise and their meaning clarified. As most of the required investments had already been completed and recorded during this period, this data formed the basis for the cost calculations. These costs represent the actual costs incurred as part of the project. Costs that had not yet been recorded by the time of data review were taken from the offers of service providers and third-party suppliers for the respective cost items. These were also included in the cost calculations at their respective values, as they were very likely to be incurred and therefore had to be taken into account.

## 3.3.2 Data Analysis

### 3.3.2.1 Individual and Total Costs

The calculations were based on the costs incurred during the project, covering the period from October 2017 to March 2020. These were recorded as part of cost type accounting and systematically categorized by topic. They represent the actual costs.

After the actual project-related costs were systematically recorded, a cost forecast was then made with a view to expanding the TNA system as part of standard care in the V-G district. In this process, not only were central system components added, but existing structures and processes from the project were also restructured to adapt them to the new requirements of standard care. The results of the actual cost analysis were thus adjusted with relevant information from project experience, and the incurred cost values were averaged. These "new costs" reflect the normal costs. The results of this analysis were generalized and ultimately represented in a planned cost function. In this context, the variable factors influencing the different cost types were defined and included as variables in the cost function.

Due to the various steps in the cost analysis described above, the presentation of results was multi-stage. First, the actual costs for the introduction and implementation of the TNA system are described based on the project results. Next, the normal costs are presented under the assumption of standard care, and finally, the planned cost function for the introduction of a TNA system, regardless of the region considered, is defined.

The classification by cost types was primarily based on the timing of payment. A distinction was made between single-period and multi-period costs. In addition, the multi-period costs were assigned to personnel costs and material costs according to business management standards. Thus, in line with the business management principles described in Sect. 2.1, three cost types were defined: one-time material costs, annual material costs, and annual personnel costs. Within the cost types, costs were categorized thematically to ensure later practical relevance to the system components of the TNA system.

One-time material costs were defined in this study as all costs and intangible investments incurred that do not count as annual personnel costs. Intangible investments reflect the costs of staff training. These are generally also defined as investments during the introduction phase, as comprehensive training of "core staff" during the implementation of the TNA system is considered a one-time cost. However, the know-how acquired by employees through training is directly tied to individuals and is therefore difficult to measure. All investments were allocated annually on a straight-line depreciation basis, as staff turnover was to be expected.

The annual material costs reflect expenses incurred for goods, which, however, have a multi-period character, such as annually recurring costs for the operational readiness of system components or consumables. In addition to the annual material costs, annual personnel costs are incurred for the new professional groups (e.g., TNA).

In addition to presenting the individual costs of each cost item, the total costs were also summarized. Since the cost presentation was to be on an annual basis, but the project only started in October 2017, costs were calculated for 12 months starting from October of each year. This approach prevented the need for a separate presentation for the first three months of 2017, which would otherwise have resulted in disproportionately high average total costs. In the results section, both individual and total costs are therefore reported separately for the first, second, third year, and so on. The described procedure was applied consistently in all subsequent analyses.

***The TNA system within the project framework until March 2020***

When introducing the TNA system as part of the Land|Rettung project, many system components were provided by the TNA system service provider. The breakdown of costs by individual system components was not apparent for all costs shown in controlling, as in some cases operator flat rates were specified for several system components. The allocation of costs to the individual cost items was carried out evenly.

Investments were depreciated on a straight-line basis, in accordance with the legally specified service lives from the tables for generally usable fixed assets (AfA tables). Table 3.3 provides an overview of the relevant data.

For salary calculations, the salaries of the professional groups paramedic, senior physician, administrative staff, and tele-emergency doctor were determined.

**Table 3.3** Overview of service lives of one-time material costs. *Source*[4]

| *One-time material costs* | *Service life in years* |
|---|---|
| *Telemedicine hardware RTW* | 5 |
| *Training hardware* | 5 |
| *Network infrastructure (hoster)* | 5 |
| *Tele-emergency physician workstation* | |
| *– Hardware and software* | 5 |
| *– Furniture* | 10 |
| *Staff training* | 4 |
| *Quality management system* | 5 |
| *Network infrastructure setup* | 5 |
| *Training materials* | 5 |

Staffing within the project, especially for the medical service of the tele-emergency physician, was highly individualized. Qualifications ranged from junior doctors to specialists and senior physicians. Due to the specific staffing of the TNA positions, the calculation of telemedicine salaries was based on the actual costs incurred for this professional group within the project. For the first year, an average salary was derived from the expenditures of the municipal emergency medical services. Personnel costs for the other professional groups were also taken from the controlling data of the municipal emergency medical services for the duration of the project.

All training sessions within the TNA system during the project period were conducted by the system's external service provider. In the controlling records of the municipal emergency medical services, only a quarterly flat rate for training costs was specified. In total, six different types of training were distinguished: initial training for emergency medical technicians and paramedics, training of multipliers and supervisors as well as tele-emergency physicians, training for control center staff, and information sessions for on-call emergency physicians. The costs for training the individual professional groups were also not directly apparent in the offers. Therefore, training costs for each professional group were calculated based on the number of person-hours incurred. The basis for this was the flat-rate costs incurred by the municipal emergency medical services as well

[4] See §193ff AO, §7 Abs 1 EStGS. 2 ff.

as the training offer from the TNA system service provider, in which the schedule and scope of each training were defined in hours. To calculate the cost per trainee for each professional group, the training duration in hours per person and professional group as well as the number of training participants per group were first determined. This allowed the total number of training hours planned by the TNA system service provider for each professional group to be calculated. The average cost per training hour for each professional group was then determined by dividing the total flat-rate cost by the sum of all training hours across all groups. This resulted in a constant cost rate per training hour. The calculated cost per trained person was obtained by multiplying the hourly rate by the planned number of training hours per person for each professional group.

***The TNA system in routine care from April 2020***

The implementation of the TNA system in the district of V-G was carried out until March 2020 as part of a research project funded by the Innovation Fund. Prehospital emergency medical routine care is subject to legal requirements. In the event of a system expansion, the current equipment in the district of V-G, based on the project measures implemented, is not sufficient to ensure routine operations. Therefore, the required cost items first had to be reassessed and, in most cases, expanded in scope, and missing system components had to be added. There was ongoing communication with the project managers of the medical evaluation and the head of the municipal emergency medical services to ensure the most realistic estimate possible of the projected resource requirements. Costs for new system components that needed to be added were supplemented based on offers from system providers.

The salary calculations from the fourth year of analysis onward were recalculated and adjusted to reflect the current collective bargaining agreements. Since there are significant differences in salaries both between occupational groups and among various qualifications within a single group (e.g., among physicians), separate imputed salary calculations were conducted as part of the cost analyses. These calculations are based on the collective agreement of University Medicine Greifswald (UMG) as well as the collective agreements for the public sector (TVöD) from 2017 to 2021 (senior physician (TN-UMN Ä3), paramedic (TVöD-P8), and administrative officer (TVöD VKA E11)). For all data unknown at the time of calculation, a steady annual wage increase of three percent was assumed.

After the end of the project, staff training was not conducted exclusively by the TNA system service provider, but is intended to be carried out to a large extent internally within the district in the future. The new training concepts were developed by the project manager in consultation with the emergency

Gross monthly employee salary (incl. annual 3% pay rise) x 12

\+ annual special payment

= Annual average employee gross salary

\+ employer's insurance contribution (23.5%)

\+ 5% UMG personnel contribution

= Annual average employer gross salary

/ (12*average number of hours per month)

**= Hourly average employer gross salary**

**Fig. 3.9** Calculation of the employer's daily gross wage. *Source* Own illustration

medical services operator. For internal district training, in addition to the opportunity costs of lost working time for trainees, the opportunity costs of lost working time for trainers must also be considered, since no personnel were specifically allocated for conducting the training and it would have to take place during regular working hours. With regard to the various cost components, it becomes clear that the labor costs of individual occupational groups are accounted for on an hourly basis in the calculations. Therefore, the employer's gross wage per hour for the relevant occupational groups had to be determined. The procedure for these calculations is shown in Fig. 3.9. The average working hours per month are derived from the average annual working days, which were calculated taking into account weekends, public holidays, vacation, sick days, and training days.

Based on the specific labor costs, the training costs per person can be calculated and easily adjusted to the required number of staff to be trained. In addition to the employee's monthly gross wage, annual special payments, employer's insurance contributions, and a 5% flat rate for providing staff for "non-core" work as TNA also had to be taken into account.

#### 3.3.2.2 Development of a Standard Cost Function

The individual and total costs broken down in Sect. 1.3.2.1 will be consolidated into a total cost function in the following chapter. The aim of the cost function is to enable calculation of the average total costs for the introduction of a TNA system in any region structurally similar to the model region, given the relevant variable values.

For this purpose, the cost types incurred in the Land|Rettung project are grouped and relevant variables are defined accordingly. Here, the cost types are regrouped according to the dependent variable. The variables represent influencing factors that may vary in magnitude depending on the region and can thus significantly affect the costs. The following explanations in this chapter are based on the publication by Prasser C. et al. (2020).

The average total costs (K) indicate the costs that would be incurred when introducing a TNA system. The following influencing factors (variables) are conceivable: number of ambulances to be retrofitted (x), number of TNA workstations (a), number of required staff per staff category i ($p^i$), and number of persons to be trained annually by staff group i ($s^i$).

The total costs are formed by adding the five cost groups: one-time material costs ($C_I$), annual personnel costs ($C_{II}$), annual operating costs ($C_{III}$), variable training costs ($C_{IV}$), and one-time material costs for ambulance equipment ($C_V$).

$$K\left(a; p^i; s^i; x\right) = C_I(a) + C_{II}\left(p^i\right) + C_{III}(a; x) + C_{IV}\left(s^i\right) + C_V(x) \quad (3.1)$$

where

| | |
|---|---|
| $K$ | total costs of the TNA system per year [€] |
| $C_I$ | One-time material costs [€] |
| $a$ | Number of TNA workstations |
| $C_{II}$ | Annual personnel costs [€] |
| $p^i$ | Number of FTE positions in staff group i |
| $C_{III}$ | Annual operating costs [€] |
| $x$ | Number of advanced life support ambulances with TNA equipment |
| $C_{IV}$ | Variable training costs [€] |
| $s^i$ | Annual number of persons to be trained by staff group i |
| $C_V$ | One-time material costs for ambulance equipment |

The *one-time material costs* include all investments required for equipping a TNA workstation as well as for the procurement and installation of the software. The number of TNA workstations to be set up (a) is decisive for the amount of these costs. The investment costs are incorporated into the cost function taking into account the standard depreciation periods according to the current AfA table.

The *annual personnel costs* consist of the costs for the tele-emergency physician as well as administrative staff, and are defined by the number of required FTE positions per staff group ($p_i$).

In addition, *annual operating costs* arise for the use and maintenance of the system. These costs depend on the number of TNA workstations in operation (a) as well as the number of advanced life support ambulances in operation (x).

To ensure correct and efficient use of the system, all staff groups must be trained. These *training costs* are represented by the cost item of variable training costs, which primarily depend on the annual number of persons to be trained ($s^i$).

The final cost item, the one-time *material costs for ambulance equipment*, consists of the one-time material costs for retrofitting the TNA ambulances and depends on the number of advanced life support ambulances to be equipped (x).

## 3.4 Centralization versus Decentralization

If the idea of transferring the TNA system is further developed, the question arises as to whether the TNA service could be conceived as a central, perhaps even nationwide, TNA center, and whether this might be more resource-efficient. This question has already been examined in the publication by Fleßa et al. (2020) "Telemedical emergency services: central or decentral coordination?". The publication addresses the feasibility as well as the advantages and disadvantages of a centralized TNA service in the routine care of the district V-G, based on the data that also underlie this dissertation. Three central questions were investigated for this purpose:

(1) What is the probability that an incoming call cannot be answered and thus enters a kind of waiting queue?
(2) How many tele-emergency physicians would have to work in parallel in a TNA center, and how many regions (e.g., districts) could then be served together? (Assumption: same quality and safety of care in both organizational forms (centralized and decentralized))
(3) Does the centralized TNA service offer cost advantages?

The basic model of a queue was already introduced in Sect. 2.5. In the TNA system, calls from emergency personnel on site represent the customers who arrive at the queuing system (the TNA control center). The system has k parallel service channels (tele-emergency physicians), and a customer does not have to wait if at least one service channel is available. Only when all channels are occupied does an incoming call from a paramedic have to wait and is placed in the queue. In order to answer the research questions, the values of the central model variables and the fundamental model structure must be known. The parameters of the model will now be defined again in the context of the TNA service, referring to the notation already introduced:

*Distribution of interarrival times (A):* How many calls arrive within a defined time period, and what is their distribution? Calls from paramedics reach the TNA control center at a rate of λ (calls per hour). The arrivals—in this system, the telephone calls—can be described by the Poisson distribution and can be represented by a Markov process.[5]

*Distribution of service times (B):* How long does a service take, and how is this time statistically distributed? It has been shown that most service times (the time during which emergency personnel on site are supported by the TNA via telephone) follow a negative exponential distribution.[6]

*Number of service stations (c):* The number of parallel channels indicates how many customers (calls from emergency personnel) can be served simultaneously by a tele-emergency physician. This value is not technically limited and is therefore assumed to be infinite.

*System capacity (n):* It can be assumed that the system capacity is infinite, since the emergency personnel on site (emergency medical technicians, paramedics, or emergency physicians) belong to the same emergency call system and wait until the TNA can take the call. (There is no alternative here; the emergency service staff must wait until the TNA answers the call.)

---

[5] See Zimmermann (2008), p. 410.

[6] See Fleßa et al. (2021), p. 3.

*Number of possible customers (v):* Here, the concept of the TNA system itself defines the value. An infinite number of customers (calls) can be assumed, since the tele-emergency physician can, in principle, be alerted to any emergency incident that arises.

*Queue discipline (s):* It is assumed that calls are answered in the order in which the TNA is alerted, and thus generally follow the first-in-first-out discipline (i.e., cases are processed in sequence).

For arrivals, it is assumed that the number of calls follows a Poisson distribution, which means that arrivals can be represented by a Markov process. The average arrival rate (per hour) is calculated by dividing the number of cases by the number of hours considered. For example, if the tele-emergency physician is on duty only from Monday to Friday for 8 hours each day, the number of hours considered would be the product of the number of days (e.g., five days) and the number of hours per day (e.g., eight hours). For 250 emergency calls during this period, the average arrival rate would be $250/5*8 = 6.25$ cases per hour.

Furthermore, each tele-emergency physician can be engaged in up to m emergencies simultaneously. Assuming that n tele-emergency physicians are working in parallel at a control center, $k = m \cdot n$ channels are available. The contact between the ambulance crew and the tele-emergency doctor can generally be described as $60/\mu$ minutes. Here, $\mu$ denotes the service rate, i.e., the number of calls that can be handled per hour. The service rate is determined based on the average mission duration per hour. If a customer is served for an average of 120 seconds, the service rate per second is $1/120 = 0.0083$. To obtain the service rate per hour, this result must be divided by 3600 (1 hour = 1 second/ 60*60). It is assumed that the service time for customer *i* is independent of the service time for customer j. Thus, the service process follows a Markov process with a negative exponential distribution.[7] Since the ambulance crew and tele-emergency physicians belong to the same emergency call system, it can be assumed that they can wait until the TNA answers a call. The system capacity is therefore unlimited. In addition, the number of potential patients in the emergency care system is infinite.

[7] See Fleßa et al. (2021), p. 1 ff.

Finally, the priority of calls must be classified. In the following model description, it is assumed that the first customers are served first (first in – first out, FIFO). The medical urgency of a case is therefore not taken into account. This results in the M/M/k/∞/∞/FIFO queueing model.[8] The calculation of the parameters λ and μ is based on the telemedical mission data during the project period, excluding the six-month introductory phase, as temporary fluctuations in the use of the TNA system are to be expected due to the high degree of innovation.

The calculation of the values was based on information about the working times of the tele-emergency physician: start, end, and consultation duration. First, the consultation duration was checked for unrepresentative outliers. For example, extremely short or long consultation durations may describe individual cases but do not correspond to the distribution of other cases and would distort the results. It can be assumed that there are times when more cases occur than at other times. Therefore, based on the analysis results for the mission duration of the TNA (Sect. 4.1.4.1), it should be examined whether it might make sense to consider only the data from possible peak times for the queueing model. The calculation of arrival and departure rates is based on the included data, in particular the average mission duration of the TNA. The queueing model was ultimately programmed in Delphi as part of the publication by Fleßa et al.

The M/M/k/∞/∞/FIFO model assumes that arrivals (λ) follow a Poisson distribution and that the service rate (μ) follows an exponential distribution. The interarrival time is thus an exponentially distributed random variable. The corresponding probability density function f(x) is given in the literature as[9]

$$f(x) = \lambda e^{-\lambda x} \text{ mit } 0 \leq x \leq \infty \quad \text{und} \quad \lambda > 0 \tag{3.2}$$

With the help of the density function, the probability of any number of incoming calls within a time interval x can be determined.[10] The expected value E and standard deviation σ of an incoming call x are defined as follows

$$E(x) = \frac{1}{\lambda} \tag{3.3}$$

$$\sigma(x) = \frac{1}{\lambda} \tag{3.4}$$

[8] The model's notation is based on the principles presented in Section 2.3.

[9] See Zimmermann (2008), p. 403 ff.

[10] See Zimmermann (2008), p. 410.

Furthermore, the traffic intensity is denoted by $\rho = \frac{\lambda}{\mu}$, which represents the ratio of arrival to service rate.[11] The probability that i calls are in the system is hereafter abbreviated as $w_i$. The fundamental formula for calculating the probability in the present model is[12]

$$w_0 = \frac{1}{\sum_{i=0}^{k-1} \frac{1}{i!} \cdot \rho^i + \frac{\rho^k}{k! \cdot \left(1 - \frac{\rho}{k}\right)}} = \frac{1}{\sum_{i=0}^{mn-1} \frac{1}{i!} \cdot \rho^i + \frac{\rho^{mn}}{(mn)! \cdot \left(1 - \frac{\rho}{mn}\right)}} \quad (3.5)$$

$$w_i = \frac{1}{i!} \rho^i w_0 \quad \text{für } i < m \cdot n \quad (3.6)$$

$$w_i = \frac{1}{k! \cdot k^{(i-k)}} \rho^i w_0 = \frac{1}{(mn)! \cdot (mn)^{(n-i)}} \rho^i w_0 \quad \text{für } i < m \cdot n \quad (3.7)$$

with

| | |
|---|---|
| $\rho$ | traffic intensity |
| $\lambda$ | arrival rate [incoming calls per hour] |
| $\mu$ | service rate [calls processed per hour] |
| $k$ | number of parallel call handlings by the on-duty TNA |
| $m$ | maximum number of calls a TNA can handle in parallel |
| $n$ | number of tele-emergency physicians in the telemedical practice |
| $\sigma$ | standard deviation of the number of completed calls per hour |
| $w_i$ | probability that i calls are in the system |

Using formula (16), the probability that a call has to wait can be given as P (i > k). Here, the number of calls *i* is greater than the number of calls handled *k* by a tele-emergency physician. This situation is defined as "system overload," in which a paramedic's call cannot be answered immediately and is placed in the queue.

$$P(i > k) = 1 - P(i \leq k) = 1 - \sum_{0}^{k} w_i \quad (3.8)$$

[11] See Hedtstück (2013), p. 196 f.

[12] See Meyer und Hansen (1996), p. 249 f.

To answer the third research question, the costs incurred also had to be calculated. The decisive factors were those costs that differed between the alternatives of a centralized or decentralized expansion of the system. System costs that were independent of the telemedical workstation could be neglected, as they did not differ between the alternatives. Likewise, the costs per TNA-RTW could be disregarded, as these were also independent of the type of telemedical service. Thus, only the costs incurred exclusively for the operation of the TNA office were relevant. Based on the preceding chapters, the cost functions for both alternatives were ultimately determined and compared for the costs per region. In addition to the centralized service, the costs for the decentralized alternative with six out of 26 RTWs (project status) as well as 26 out of 26 RTWs were also analyzed.

# Results 4

## 4.1 Deployment Statistics

### 4.1.1 Trends in Deployment Numbers

*General Case Number Trends*

All available mission data from January 2015 through February 2020 were cleaned according to the methodology described in Sect. 3.2.2. In total, 177,674 RTW and 81,431 NEF deployments were available as raw data records. During the cleaning process, 4% of RTW and 4.8% of NEF raw data were excluded from further analysis due to duplication or insufficient plausibility. After cleaning, 170,720 RTW records remained, of which 149,751 were primary deployments and 20,969 were secondary deployments. Cleaning of the NEF data resulted in 75,526 primary and 2033 secondary deployments for the entire observation period. Due to structural developments in the district, there were a total of 37 RTW and 19 NEF units over the entire observation period. It should be noted, however, that some response units were replaced or newly acquired at the stations over the years. The total number also includes reserve vehicles, which are only deployed when the regular response unit is unavailable or when demand for medical services changes.

Before the mission data are analyzed in detail, an overview of the development of deployment numbers over the entire pre-post observation period will be provided.

The trend in RTW mission data over time is shown in Fig. 4.1. Despite seasonal fluctuations, there is an overall slight increase in the number of primary deployments. The number of secondary deployments appears to fluctuate only slightly over a longer period. However, a significant increase is observed in the



R. Süss, *The Tele-Emergency Physician System as an Innovation in Prehospital Emergency Care*, https://doi.org/10.1007/978-3-658-49561-9_4

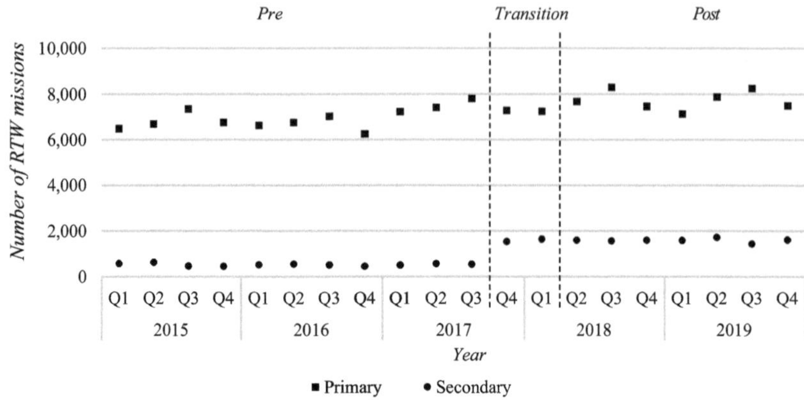


**Fig. 4.1** RTW mission data over time. *Source* Own representation

fourth quarter of 2017. Deployments from the first two months of 2020 are not included in the figure, as they do not represent a full quarter and would have distorted the presentation.

For a total of 77,559 cleaned records, an NEF was indicated in the identifier (column FKENNER) (both primary and secondary). In contrast to RTW deployments, there is a slight decline in primary NEF deployments (see Fig. 4.2). In 2015, an average of 4000 deployments per quarter were accompanied by an NEF. By 2019, this average had dropped to just 3500 deployments per quarter with an NEF on site. The number of secondary NEF deployments has increased slightly over the years.

Figure 4.3 shows the telemedical mission data from the introduction of the system onward.

In the post-phase, between 272 and 481 TNA primary deployments occurred per quarter. The number of secondary deployments fluctuated between 5 and 11 per quarter. In comparison, the transition phase saw fewer primary deployments and a similar number of secondary deployments. Appendix 1 in the electronic supplementary material provides a tabular overview of the development of deployment numbers by quarter and year for the vehicle types RTW, NEF, and TNA.

Between the fourth quarter of 2017 and February 2020, there were 3611 TNA activations. When analyzing only the post-period, there were 3019 activations. As previously described in detail, the mission data were methodologically linked with the RTW mission data for the observation period. Each year, between 7 and

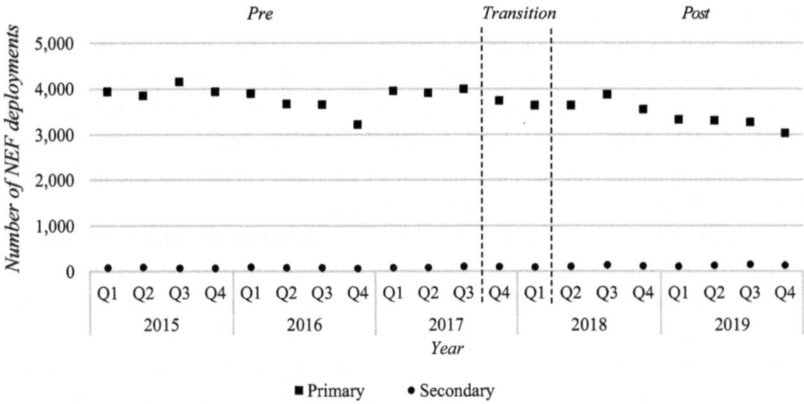


**Fig. 4.2** NEF mission data over time. *Source* Own representation

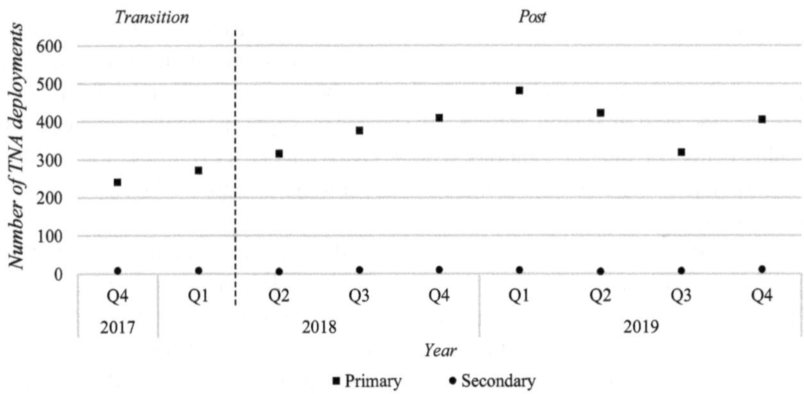


**Fig. 4.3** TNA mission data over time. *Source* Own representation

33 TNA deployments could not be assigned to an RTW deployment. This was often due to technical issues that resulted in offline deployments, where neither the deployment number from the emergency medical services software nor the vehicle identifier could be transferred to the system. Ultimately, the number of assignable TNA deployments was 3516 (3437 primary and 79 secondary).

*Deployments by Station*

For the analysis by station, as described in Sect. 3.2.3, the periods from the second quarter of 2015 to the fourth quarter of 2016 and analogously from the second quarter of 2018 to the fourth quarter of 2019 were considered. The following analysis differentiates between RTW and NEF stations as well as primary and secondary deployments. An overview of all results presented can be found in Appendix 2 of the electronic supplementary material.

Deployment numbers in the interval under consideration increased from an average of 6513 deployments per quarter in the pre-period to an average of 7776 deployments per quarter in the post-period. In the pre-interval, the highest proportion of primary deployments was in Greifswald by RTW Station 4 (15.1%) and RTW Station 5 (13.5%). Relatively few primary deployments were handled by RTW Stations 6 (1.4%), 13 (2%), 12 (2.6%), and Stations 2 and 3 (each with 3%). The post-phase presents a different picture. While RTW Stations 4 and 5 (14.1% and 13.2%) and Station 1 (8.5%) still lead, other stations with high deployment volumes now include Station 3 (7.4%), Station 17 (7.3%), and Station 19 (6.8%).

A detailed analysis of unit involvement at the district's 21 RTW stations showed that many stations experienced a slight decrease in the percentage of primary deployment participation, fluctuating between −0.1% and −1.5% from pre- to post-period. Only Station 19 showed a slight percentage increase in deployments per quarter. Stations with a TNA-capable RTW did not show disproportionately high or low changes compared to other stations, but all showed a decrease in RTW deployments.

The analysis of NEF stations was conducted in the same manner. The average quarterly deployment volume (primary) declined slightly from the pre- (3835) to the post-period (3428). In the pre-interval, most deployments were accompanied by NEF Station 5 (14.6%), Station 6 (14.8%), Station 3 (9.9%), and Station 1 (9.6%). The post-survey period shows a similar pattern. Here, too, the NEFs at the aforementioned stations had the highest deployment accompaniment, though almost all saw a slight decrease. The lowest average deployments per quarter in both periods were at NEF Stations 4, 7, and 9. Looking at the pre-post comparison, only marginal changes are observed, with fluctuations ranging from −1.1% to +1.8% for individual stations. Stations that were closed, newly opened, or relocated during the observation period were not considered, as these would have shown the greatest changes.

The NEF secondary deployments are predominantly carried out in both the pre- and post-phase by the NEF units at stations 13 (40.2% and 40.5%), station 1 (17.9% and 16.1%), and station 11 (13.1% and 10.5%). The fewest deployments per quarter in both scenarios are recorded at station 7 (0.1% and 0.3%), station 4 (0.2% each), and station 9 (0.9% each). Overall, the average number of quarterly deployments increased from 85 in the pre-period to 125 in the post-period.

Furthermore, it was observed that NEF stations located in the northern part of the district, and thus closer to the retrofitted TNA-RTW sites, experienced a general decrease in NEF deployments during the post-interval.

*False alarms*

In addition to the overall analysis of deployment numbers, a distinction between deployments and false alarms will be made later, particularly with regard to response times. At this point, the basic trend in false alarms over the three observation periods is presented. Since the analysis is not conducted on a quarterly basis, the deployment numbers from January and February 2020 are included. Table 4.1 provides an overview.

The rate of inappropriate deployments for primary ambulance (RTW) missions has remained largely unchanged from 2015 to 2020, at 18.6%. In contrast, the proportion of secondary inappropriate deployments has decreased from 2.4% to 1.5%. In the pre-phase, 9.5% of primary missions by ground-based emergency physicians were classified as inappropriate deployments. This proportion temporarily increased by 2% during the transition phase. However, in the post-phase, the proportion of inappropriate deployments fell again to 10.2%, which is still 0.7% above the initial value in the pre-phase. Here as well, the percentage of inappropriate deployments in secondary cases has declined. In a pre-post comparison, the proportion decreased from 7.7% to 6.5%.

In the post-phase, the proportion of telemedical inappropriate deployments is 14.4% for primary missions and 8.8% for secondary missions. It is important to note here that the definition of an inappropriate deployment differs between the response units RTW/NEF and TNA.

### 4.1.2 Response Time Limits

The analysis of the response time limit was initially conducted over the entire pre-post period. The results are shown in Table 4.2. As already described in the methodology, there are sometimes large differences in the number of deployments from pre to post. The results in the table are based on all primary deployment data for the entire V-G district.

The response times from alert to arrival at the scene are considered. The evaluation of the HF column does not differentiate between the first, second, third,

**Table 4.1** Proportion of inappropriate deployments overall. *Source* Own representation

| | Primary | | | Secondary | | |
|---|---|---|---|---|---|---|
| | Pre | Transition | Post | Pre | Transition | Post |
| **RTW** | | | | | | |
| Number of missions | 62,169 | 11,820 | 47,894 | 5,645 | 3119 | 11,839 |
| Number of inappropriate deployments | 14,226 | 2701 | 10,941 | 138 | 49 | 179 |
| Proportion of inappropriate deployments [%] | 18.6 | 18.6 | 18.6 | 2.4 | 1.5 | 1.5 |
| **NEF** | | | | | | |
| Number of missions | 38,194 | 6538 | 23,334 | 831 | 183 | 879 |
| Number of inappropriate deployments | 3987 | 838 | 2636 | 69 | 10 | 61 |
| Proportion of inappropriate deployments [%] | 9.5 | 11.4 | 10.2 | 7.7 | 5.2 | 6.5 |
| **TNA** | | | | | | |
| Number of missions | | 533 | 2992 | | 18 | 62 |
| Number of inappropriate deployments | | 56 | 503 | | 5 | 6 |
| Proportion of inappropriate deployments [%] | | 9.5 | 14.4 | | 21.7 | 8.8 |

**Table 4.2** Parameters of the response time limit for primary deployments. *Source* Own representation, [mean (MW), standard deviation (SD), median (MD)]

| Response unit | Pre | | | | Post | | | |
|---|---|---|---|---|---|---|---|---|
| | Number of deployments | Mean [mm:ss] | SD [mm:ss] | MD [mm:ss] | Number of deployments | Mean [mm:ss] | SD [mm:ss] | MD [mm:ss] |
| RTW | 76,395 | 9:49 | 10:13 | 08:00 | 58,852 | 10:19 | 17:37 | 08:00 |
| NEF | 42,181 | 10:18 | 10:20 | 08:00 | 25,975 | 10:36 | 15:39 | 09:00 |

etc. arriving vehicle. On average, the pre-response time limit for the ambulance (RTW) is 9:49 ± 10:13 min (mean ± SD). This value increases to 10:19 ± 17:37 min in the post period. The median response time in both intervals is 8 min. When identifying outliers using the interquartile range between the first and third quartile, it is noticeable that the upper limit for outliers is already at a response time limit of 23.5 min for both observation intervals. Thus, 3.6% and 3.7% of deployments in the pre- and post-periods, respectively, are defined as outliers, as they do not correspond to the typical distribution of the other deployments.

For the NEF, the mean response times are 10:18 ± 10:20 min in the pre-period and 10:36 ± 15:39 min in the post-period. The median increased by one minute from pre to post.

### 4.1.3 Participation Rates of Emergency Physicians

For the pre-period, the participation rates of the NEF, initially regardless of the TNA, in primary and secondary deployments were calculated from the datasets of the emergency medical services software. Of the total 74,696 emergency calls in the pre-period, at least one NEF was additionally dispatched in 42,078 cases, resulting in a participation rate of 56.3%. The participation rate of the emergency physician in secondary missions is 15.2%. The data for the post-period were evaluated using the same methodology. Here, the NEF participation rate in primary deployments is 44.1%. Thus, the rate decreased by 12.2%. In secondary deployments as well, the proportion of ground-based emergency physicians is no longer as high as in the pre-period. The rate is 7.5%.

Next, the proportion of ambulance deployments involving a tele-emergency physician was determined. This varies greatly depending on the response unit. However, if only the retrofitted TNA ambulances are considered, the proportions range between 15.3% and 22.2% depending on the ambulance. Across all TNA ambulance deployments, the average utilization of the tele-emergency physician is 18% for deployments since the system was introduced.

Finally, a brief analysis was conducted of the columns "type of deployment" and "incident type" from the TNA deployment data sheet. The analysis of the 3060 telemedical mission data showed that in over 72% of all TNA deployments, no emergency physician was additionally dispatched at the beginning of the deployment. In 147 deployments (4.8%), the emergency physician was en route or was subsequently dispatched, with the tele-emergency physician handing over the deployment to the on-site emergency physician in 139 cases. This corresponds to a rate of 4.5% in relation to the total number of TNA deployments in the post-period. In contrast, the tele-emergency physician took over only twelve deployments from the emergency physician (0.4%). In 25 cases, either the general practitioner or a representative of the on-call medical service was already at the scene when the TNA was consulted.

### 4.1.4 Deployment Times

#### 4.1.4.1 TNA Deployments

As already shown in Sect. 3.2.3, individual parameters of the incident distribution of the tele-emergency physician in the post-phase of the project are first presented.

The post-observation period covers 700 days. The maximum number of deployments per day was 15, which occurred only once. Most frequently, there were 4 TNA deployments per day (144 times). Considering all telemedical deployments, the average was 4.4 deployments per day. Most deployments occurred on Fridays (16% of all deployments), Tuesdays (13%), and Saturdays (10%). On the remaining weekdays, only between 5% and 7% of TNA alerts occurred.

A total of 41 missions could not be included in the analysis due to missing time data, resulting in 3019 mission data from the post-period available for analysis. The analysis of telemedical missions further showed that most TNA activations occur between 9 and 10 a.m. Figure 4.4 provides an overview of the distribution of missions. The decisive factor for categorization was the time at the

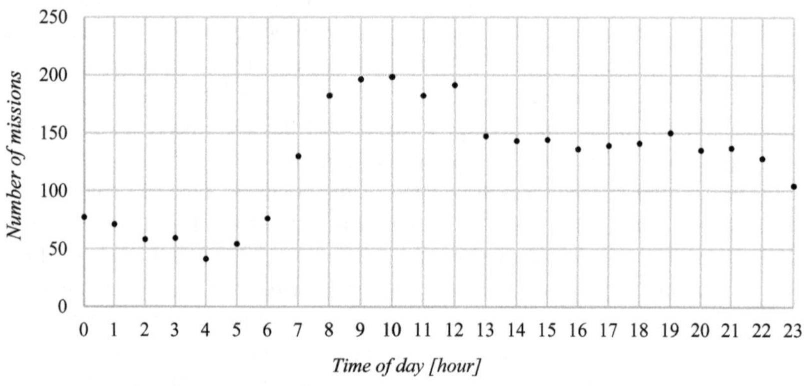


**Fig. 4.4** Distribution of TNA missions by time of day. *Source* Own illustration

start of a TNA activation. Between midnight and 6 a.m., there were comparatively few missions compared to the rest of the day.

Figure 4.4 shows the involvement of the tele-emergency physician in terms of consultation duration across the distribution of missions by time-of-day categories. Each time-of-day category covers a four-hour interval. The first time interval was set to start at 8 a.m., as this marks the beginning of the 24-hour shift for a TNA. It is immediately apparent that nearly 28% of all missions took place between 8 and 11 a.m., with 62% having a consultation duration of 0 to 15 minutes. The percentage distribution of consultation durations is very similar across all time-of-day categories. At all times of day, the consultation duration is on average 0 to 15 minutes in 59% of missions within a time-of-day category, 16 to 30 minutes in 25%, 31 to 45 minutes in 11%, and over 46 minutes in 5% of missions (see Fig. 4.5).

The use of tele- and video communication enables the TNA to be involved in more than one mission simultaneously. For example, during a lengthy transfer that does not require high-level acute medical care, the TNA can also supervise another mission. However, the decision to take on additional, parallel cases always rests with the individual judgment of the on-duty tele-emergency physician. In the post-period, a total of 63 missions took place in parallel. Figure 4.6 shows the distribution of parallel missions by start time and time of day. A parallel mission at 1 a.m. thus indicates that there was a temporal overlap of two telemedical missions between 01:00 and 01:59. The figure shows a marked increase

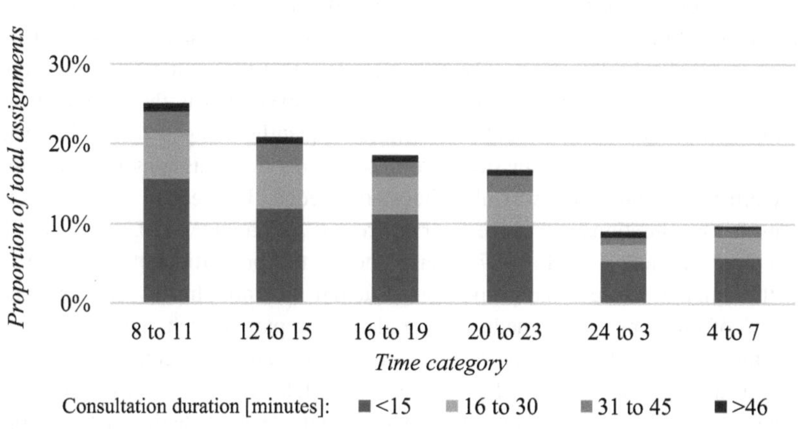


**Fig. 4.5** TNA incident distribution by time of day and consultation duration. *Source* Own illustration

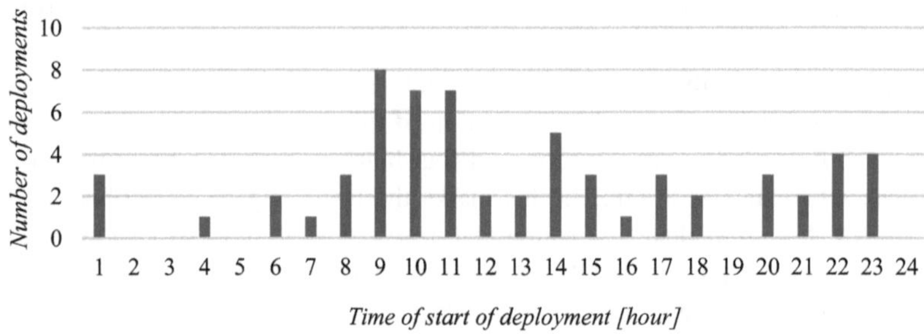


**Fig. 4.6** Distribution of parallel missions by time of day. *Source* Own illustration

in parallel missions between 9 and 11 a.m., with a maximum of eight parallel missions. Between midnight and 8 a.m., there were comparatively fewer parallel missions.

With regard to the distribution of parallel missions by day of the week, it is noticeable that most parallel missions (16 missions) occurred on Fridays. Parallel missions were also more frequent on Tuesdays (13 missions) and Saturdays (10 missions) than on other days of the week.

The initial data analysis showed that a particularly large number of missions had very short consultation and conversation times. The mission data from the transition phase are not included in these calculations.

The frequency distribution of consultation duration by time interval is shown in Fig. 4.7. In the analysis of this parameter, eight missions had no value. These were telemedical false alarms. Overall, it is clear that the frequency of missions decreases as consultation duration increases. An exception is the interval from 6 to 10 minutes. At 26%, the TNA is most frequently engaged in this interval. However, 12.8% of these missions are false alarms, i.e., missions in which the tele-emergency physician was ultimately not needed. The second most frequent consultation durations are in the interval from 0 to 5 minutes (20.2% of all telemedical missions). As Fig. 4.7 clearly shows, the proportion of false alarms in this interval exceeds the proportion of actual missions. In this time interval, 56.2% of missions are telemedical false alarms. In particular, it can be observed that the number of false alarms decreases as mission duration increases.

On average, across all deployments, the tele-emergency physician was engaged for $17 \pm 15$ minutes per deployment, with 50% of deployments lasting less than 11 minutes. The longest mission duration exceeded three hours. The distinction between false calls and actual deployments confirms the observation that

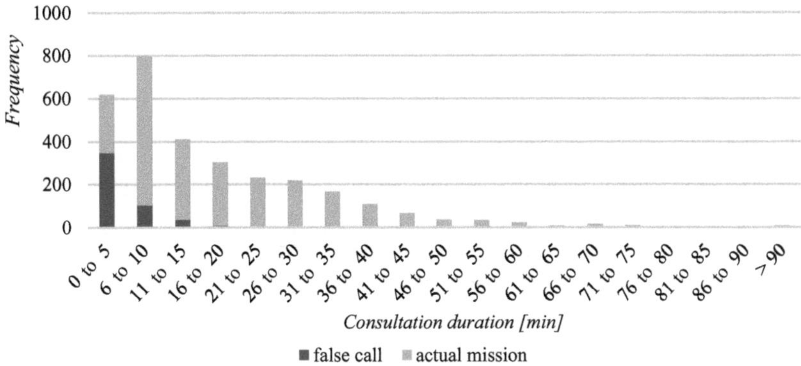


**Fig. 4.7** Frequency distribution of TNA consultation duration. *Source* Own illustration

**Table 4.3** Statistical parameters of consultation duration by type of deployment. *Source* Own representation, [Mean (MW), Standard deviation (SD), Minimum (Min), Maximum (Max), Median (MD)]

| | MW [min] | SD [min] | Min [min] | Max [min] | MD [min] |
|---|---|---|---|---|---|
| **Total TNA deployments** | 17 | 15 | 0 | 195 | 11 |
| *of which false call* | 4 | 8 | 0 | 118 | 0 |
| *of which actual mission* | 19 | 15 | 0 | 195 | 15 |

the TNA is engaged for a significantly shorter period in a false call, at 4 ± 8 minutes, compared to an actual deployment (19 ± 15 minutes). The median also supports this statement when comparing both values. The results are summarized in Table 4.3.

The second time parameter available from the telemedicine data was the conversation duration (= cumulative conversation time between the ambulance crew and the TNA during a deployment). The effect of short false calls, already observed in the consultation duration, is even more pronounced here (see Fig. 4.8). Most cumulative conversation times (15.2%) between the two parties lasted 0 to 1 minute. In this interval, there are 3.3 times as many false calls as actual deployments. The number of false calls also decreases sharply as conversation duration increases. The longest cumulative conversation duration recorded was 30 minutes. In most deployments (6.5%), the TNA was engaged in conversations lasting 8 to 9 minutes. For conversation durations over 40 minutes, only

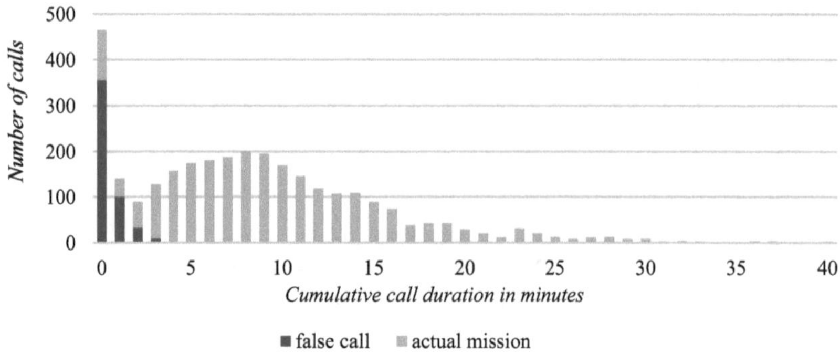


**Fig. 4.8** Frequency distribution of the cumulative conversation duration of the TNA. *Source* Own representation

isolated cases occur, which are not shown in Fig. 4.8. The longest conversation duration of 60 minutes was reached in two deployments.

On average, a telemedicine deployment is associated with a cumulative conversation time of $8 \pm 7$ minutes and a median of 8 minutes. Again, there are significant differences between actual misison and false calls. While a false call requires on average only 33 seconds of conversation time[1], the average for an actual mission is $10 \pm 7$ minutes. The results are presented in Table 4.4.

In summary, the deployment times of the TNA show that, on average, it is engaged for $19 \pm 15$ minutes per mission, with the cumulative conversation time per deployment averaging $10 \pm 7$ minutes. False alarms last an average of 4 minutes, during which the tele-emergency physician is typically in verbal contact with the ambulance crew for only a few seconds.

Up to this point, all telemedical deployments have been considered, distinguishing between false alarms and actual missions. To conclude this chapter, a brief analysis of deployment times from the perspective of primary and secondary missions is provided for comparison. Since purely consultative discussions between the advanced life support ambulance crew and the TNA are also possible, these have been included here for completeness. Table 4.5 summarizes the results. During the post-intervention period under review, there were 2992 primary missions, 62 secondary missions, and 6 consultative discussions.

[1] In Table 4.6, the value is given as 0 because it was rounded to minutes.

**Table 4.4** Statistical parameters of conversation duration by type of deployment. *Source* Own representation, [Mean (MW), Standard deviation (SD), Minimum (Min), Maximum (Max), Median (MD)]

| | MW [min] | SD [min] | Min [min] | Max [min] | MD [min] |
|---|---|---|---|---|---|
| **Total TNA deployments** | 8 | 7 | 0 | 60 | 8 |
| *of which false call* | 0 | 2 | 0 | 30 | 0 |
| *of which actual mission* | 10 | 7 | 0 | 60 | 9 |

**Table 4.5** Consultation and conversation duration by type of mission. *Source* Own representation, [Mean (MW), Standard deviation (SD), Minimum (Min), Maximum (Max), Median (MD)]

| | Mean [min] | SD [min] | Min [min] | Max [min] | Median [min] |
|---|---|---|---|---|---|
| **consultation duration** | | | | | |
| Primary | 15 | 14 | 0 | 195 | 11 |
| Secondary | 18 | 16 | 1 | 95 | 16 |
| Consultation | 21 | 7 | 12 | 29 | 14 |
| **conversation duration** | | | | | |
| Primary | 8 | 7 | 0 | 60 | 8 |
| Secondary | 7 | 8 | 0 | 40 | 8 |
| Consultation | 5 | 4 | 0 | 10 | 5 |

The results show that the tele-emergency physician is engaged slightly longer in a secondary mission ($18 \pm 16$ minutes) than in a primary mission ($15 \pm 14$ minutes). The cumulative conversation time is, on average, 1 minute longer in primary missions. The consultative discussions conducted, which do not reflect standard operational scenarios, have the longest consultation duration at 21 minutes, but the actual conversation time is the shortest at 5 minutes compared to primary and secondary missions.

#### 4.1.4.2 Ambulance and Emergency Physician Missions

The following section first describes the trends in primary missions, followed by secondary missions. The deployment times for advanced life support ambulances and emergency physician vehicles are presented in Table 4.6 as a pre-post comparison.

**Table 4.6** Pre-post comparison of deployment times for EMS and emergency physician vehicles. *Source* Own representation, [mean (MW), standard deviation (SD), median (MD)]

| | Pre | | | | Post | | | |
|---|---|---|---|---|---|---|---|---|
| | Number of missions | Mean [min] | SD [min] | Median [min] | Number of missions | Mean [min] | SD [min] | Median [min] |
| **Primary** | | | | | | | | |
| Total RTW | 76,395 | 78 | 44 | 68 | 58,835 | 80 | 45 | 70 |
| *of which with TNA* | – | – | – | – | 2924 | 86 | 40 | 78 |
| *of which without TNA* | – | – | – | – | 55,911 | 79 | 45 | 70 |
| Emergency physician vehicle | 42,181 | 60 | 36 | 51 | 25,969 | 63 | 37 | 54 |
| **Secondary** | | | | | | | | |
| Total RTW | 5783 | 118 | 67 | 106 | 12,018 | 85 | 55 | 74 |
| *of which with TNA* | – | – | – | – | 63 | 140 | 89 | 110 |
| *of which without TNA* | – | – | – | – | 11,955 | 85 | 54 | 74 |
| Emergency physician vehicle | 900 | 89 | 42 | 89 | 940 | 90 | 46 | 91 |

*Primary missions*

Advanced life support ambulances in the district were engaged for an average of 78 ± 44 minutes per mission during the pre-intervention period. The median mission duration was 68 minutes. All three key figures for mission duration increased in the post-intervention period. In the post-analysis, a distinction was also made between ambulance deployments with and without TNA involvement. It is evident that advanced life support ambulances were engaged for significantly longer on average when the tele-emergency physician was involved—86 minutes com-

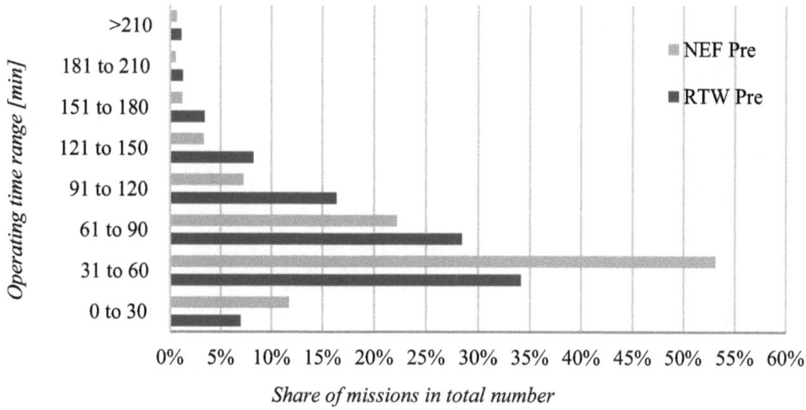


**Fig. 4.9** Frequency distribution by mission duration intervals, pre-intervention. *Source* Own representation

pared to 79 minutes without TNA involvement. The most common mission durations were between 31 and 60 minutes and between 61 and 90 minutes, as shown in Fig. 4.9. Mission durations of 91 to 120 minutes also accounted for 16.4% of the total number of ambulance deployments.

The average mission duration for emergency physician vehicles in the pre-intervention period was 60 minutes, with a standard deviation of 36 minutes. The median for all missions during this period was 51 minutes. An analysis of the mission duration categories further showed that more than half (53.1%) of the recorded emergency physician missions in the pre-intervention period had durations between 31 and 60 minutes. This was followed by durations of 61 to 90 minutes (22.2%), 0 to 30 minutes (11.7%), and 91 to 120 minutes (7.2%).

Figure 4.9 once again illustrates the previously described frequency distribution of the eight deployment time intervals, comparing NEF and RTW in the pre-intervention period. It becomes apparent that the distribution for both vehicle types is similar, although the NEF shows a higher proportion of deployments than the RTW, particularly in the 0 to 30 min and 31 to 60 min intervals. From a mission duration of 61 min onwards, the proportion of RTW deployments increases.

*Secondary deployments*

It is evident that the number of secondary deployments is consistently lower than that of primary deployments; however, the deployment times for all parameter values are higher than those for primary deployments. For example, in the

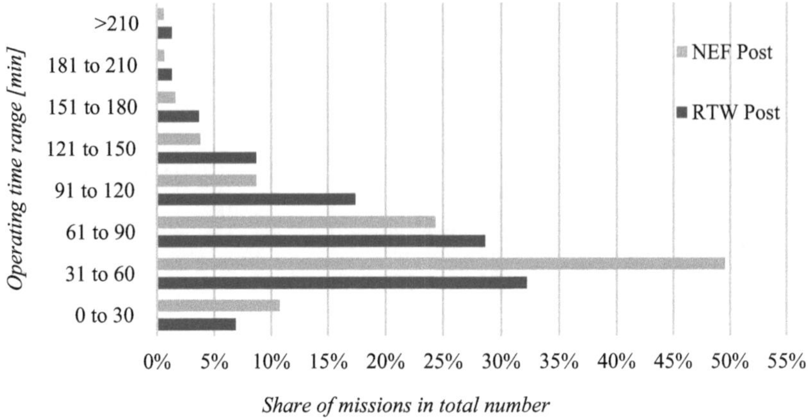


**Fig. 4.10** Frequency distribution by deployment time intervals, post-intervention. *Source* Own representation

pre-intervention period, an RTW is engaged in a deployment for an average of 118 ± 67 min, while in the post-intervention period, this is reduced to only 85 ± 55 min. Here, too, it is clear that RTWs accompanied by a TNA are engaged for longer periods (140 ± 89 min) than those without a tele-emergency physician (85 ± 54 min).

In the pre-intervention period, the NEF is engaged in a deployment for an average of 89 min, which is 29 min shorter than the RTW. This relationship changes in the post-intervention period, with the NEF now engaged for slightly longer (90 ± 46 min) than the RTW, which averages 85 ± 54 min.

As part of the post-intervention analysis, the frequency of deployments by time interval was again examined. The results are shown in Fig. 4.10. The distribution is similar to that observed in the pre-intervention situation.

The following chapter presents the deployment times of the TNA. In order to accurately analyze the effects of the TNA system at a later stage, deployment times during a false alarm must also be considered. Since the focus here is particularly on the impact on emergency physician deployments, the false alarms of the NEF are presented in detail at the end of the chapter (Table 4.7).

The table shows that the percentage of emergency physician missions changed only slightly in the pre-post comparison. The proportion of NEF primary missions decreased by 0.8% after the introduction of the TNA system. On average, since the introduction of the tele-emergency physician, the emergency physician

**Table 4.7** Parameters of NEF mission duration after false alarms. *Source* Own representation, [Mean (MW), Standard deviation (SD), Median (MD), FA (false alarms)]

| NEF | Pre | | | | Post | | | |
|---|---|---|---|---|---|---|---|---|
| | Proportion of missions [%] | Mean [min] | SD [min] | Median [min] | Proportion of missions [%] | Mean [min] | SD [min] | Median [min] |
| **Primary** | | | | | | | | |
| Actual mission | 90.5 | 61 | 35 | 52 | 89.7 | 64 | 36 | 55 |
| False call | 9.5 | 46 | 33 | 38 | 10.3 | 46 | 34 | 39 |
| **Secondary** | | | | | | | | |
| Actual mission | 92.4 | 92 | 39 | 91 | 92.9 | 93 | 55 | 93 |
| False call | 7.6 | 49 | 55 | 34 | 7.1 | 33 | 25 | 25 |

has been engaged in deployments for 3 minutes longer. For secondary missions, the proportion for the NEF increased slightly, while it decreased for secondary deployments overall.

## 4.2 Costs of the Tele-Emergency Doctor System

### 4.2.1 Status Quo in the Project

#### 4.2.1.1 Relevant Structures

First, the individual cost items will be presented below. Table 4.8 provides an overview of the cost items incurred for the TNA system in the Land|Rettung project, categorized by the type of costs incurred. To provide an overview of the necessary cost items in the TNA system, these are described below based on the central TNA system components: TNA-RTW, TNA workstation, personnel, and general system components.

*Tele-emergency doctor RTW*

Six of the 28 regular RTWs in the district were equipped with telemedicine technology as part of the project. The complex conversion and upgrade of these vehicles required both investments in technology (1) and costs for the conversion itself (5). The continuous operational readiness of an RTW also results in annual costs in the form of an operator's fee (10).

**Table 4.8** Structure of the cost calculation by cost item. *Source* Own illustration

| | Cost item | Definition |
|---|---|---|
| **One-time material costs** | | |
| 1 | Equipment per RTW | Costs for the telemedicine equipment of the RTW |
| 2 | TNA training software | Procurement of software |
| 3 | Network infrastructure | Procurement of hosting services |
| 4 | TNA workstation | Equipment and setup of the teleemergency doctor workstation |
| 5 | Conversion of TNA-RTW | Installation of telemedicine equipment in an RTW |
| 6 | Quality management system | Establishment and use |
| 7 | Network setup | Integration of computer-aided dispatch system, server, and interfaces |
| 8 | Training materials | Provision of training materials |
| 9 | Training costs | All professional groups |
| **Annual material costs** | | |
| 10 | TNA-RTW | Technical operation of the teleemergency doctor-RTW including support and maintenance, consumables |
| 11 | TNA workstation | Technical operation of the teleemergency doctor workstation as well as rental of the premises |
| 12 | Server infrastructure | Technical operation of the network infrastructure/cloud |
| 13 | Support, maintenance and security | Operator's fee |
| 14 | Quality management system | Operator's fee |
| **Annual personnel costs** | | |
| 15 | Medical service | Tele-emergency doctor and supervisor |
| 16 | Administration | Coordination and responsibility in the administrative area |

*Teleemergency doctor workstation*

The TNA requires a specially equipped workstation for telemedical consultation with the RTW personnel. Setting up this workstation with hardware (monitors, computers), an ampullarium (as is typically integrated in emergency backpacks), and office furniture results in investment costs (4). The separate room and its furnishings also lead to investment costs and annual rental expenses (11). In addition, there are annual costs for the ongoing use and operational readiness of the TNA workstation (11).

*Personnel*

The training of specialized personnel is a fundamental component. The initial training sessions conducted in the project were provided by the TNA system service provider, with different training concepts applied depending on the professional group (9). For tele-emergency doctors, multipliers, and supervisory staff, multi-day training sessions were held in Aachen, as the system had already been successfully established there by the service provider. In the context of the project, multipliers are emergency service personnel who are to provide future instruction to new emergency medical staff in the use of telemedicine technology. A supervisor, who is a specially trained tele-emergency doctor, is responsible for supervising the teleemergency doctors. So far, one tele-emergency doctor in the district has been trained as a supervisor. The training costs incurred cover the training itself as well as accommodation and travel expenses. In addition, imputed costs arise due to the loss of working hours of the personnel being trained during the training sessions.

Dispatch center operators, ground-based emergency physicians, and station staff are introduced to the new technology and its functionality on site by a representative of the service provider, usually in the form of day-long training sessions. Due to staff turnover, multiplier effects occur, so no additional costs need to be budgeted.

The service provider also supplies work materials (8). For the ongoing training of tele-emergency physicians in the district of V-G, additional investment was made in the provider's training software (2).

The medical staff (15) for the tele-emergency physician service and supervision is provided by University Medicine Greifswald. The qualifications of the part-time physicians working as tele-emergency doctors range from residents and specialists to senior physicians. This heterogeneity means that the personnel costs for the provision of TNA staff, already accounted for in the 2018 project year, form the basis for future costs (taking into account an annual 3% wage increase). The supervisor is responsible for coordinating and overseeing the medical tele-emergency physician service. Coordination and responsibility for the administrative area lies with a project officer (16).

*General system components*

The system's functionality requires various subsystems, referred to here as general system components. This includes the network infrastructure, for which a hosting provider must be set up. This incurs investment costs (3). Its integration into the computer-aided dispatch system, the connection to the fleet server, and the setup costs for the dispatch center's disposition tool for the tele-emergency physician represent one-time material costs for establishing the network infrastructure (7). In addition, a quality management system must be introduced and established, which also incurs material costs (6). To ensure the continuous operational readiness of all system components, as well as support, maintenance, and assurance, an annual operator fee is paid to the service provider (12; 13; 14).

#### 4.2.1.2 Individual Costs and Average Total Costs

The calculation of individual costs was carried out according to the methodology described in Sect. 3.3.2.1. Table 4.9 shows the costs incurred for each of the first three years of the project. These are broken down according to the cost item structure introduced in the previous chapter. The values in the "Unit price gross" column represent the costs of each item in the first year. The individual costs in the area of annual personnel expenses change over the years, but for the sake of clarity, these are not shown separately here. Depending on the frequency of the cost item (column "Quantity") and the useful lives of the assets shown in Table 3.3, the total prices for the first three years of analysis ("Total price gross") are calculated. Since the number of cost items remains the same over the years in this scenario, this column is not repeated.

It is notable that many cost items incur costs at a constant level over the years. This applies to the linear depreciation of one-time material expenditures as well as the annual operating costs of the system (annual material expenditures), which are also budgeted by the third-party provider at a constant annual rate for the duration of the project. Only personnel costs change over the years due to ongoing calculated wage increases.

The highest one-time costs are in the area of equipping the total of six ambulances with telemedicine technology, amounting to € 243,324 (= € 40,504 × 6 ambulances). The flat-rate fee charged by the service provider for training all professional groups (TNA, supervision, multipliers, mobile emergency physicians, etc.) represents the second highest cost item at € 205,000. One-time costs for the network infrastructure and the hardware equipment of the TNA workstation amount to € 47,082 and € 48,831, respectively.

**Table 4.9** Breakdown of individual costs (Project Land|Rettung). *Source* Own representation)

| | cost item | 1st year | | | 2nd year | 3rd year |
|---|---|---|---|---|---|---|
| | | Unit price gross [€] | Quantity | Total price gross [€] | Total price gross [€] | Total price gross [€] |
| **One-time material costs** | | | | | | |
| 1 | Equipment per ambulance | 40,554 | 6 | 48,664 | 48,664 | 48,664 |
| 2 | TNA training software | 27,139 | 1 | 5428 | 5428 | 5428 |
| 3 | Network infrastructure | 47,082 | 1 | 9416 | 9416 | 9416 |
| 4 | TNA workstation | 48,831 | 1 | 9766 | 9766 | 9766 |
| 5 | Conversion TNA-RTW | 6045 | 6 | 7254 | 7254 | 7254 |
| 6 | Quality management system | 19,522 | 1 | 3904 | 3904 | 3904 |
| 7 | Network setup | 36,106 | 1 | 7221 | 7221 | 7221 |
| 8 | Training materials | 557 | 1 | 139 | 139 | 139 |
| 9 | Training costs | 205,000 | 1 | 68,333 | 68,333 | 68,333 |
| **Annual material costs** | | | | | | |
| 10 | TNA-RTW | 55,147 | 6 | 330,896 | 330,896 | 330,896 |
| 11 | TNA workstation | 114,064 | 1 | 114,065 | 114,065 | 114,065 |
| 12 | Server infrastructure | 97,431 | 1 | 97,431 | 97,431 | 97,431 |
| 13 | Support, maintenance and assurance | 145,916 | 1 | 145,916 | 145,916 | 145,916 |
| 14 | Quality management system | 27,560 | 1 | 27,560 | 27,560 | 27,560 |
| **Annual personnel costs** | | | | | | |
| 15 | Medical service | 559,213 | 1 | 559,213 | 575,989 | 593,269 |
| 16 | Administration | 50,358 | 1 | 50,358 | 51,869 | 53,425 |

In the area of annual costs, operating expenses remain constant over the first three years of analysis. Within this cost category, the highest expense is incurred by the operator flat rate for the TNA-RTW (330,882 € = 55,147 € · 6 RTW).

Before presenting the total costs over the first three years of the TNA system from the district of V-G, the thematic distribution of costs by system components will first be outlined. Figure 4.11 shows the percentage distribution of total costs in the first year. The list of assigned cost items is provided in parentheses.

The costs for training and instruction of all emergency medical service personnel account for 42.8% of the total costs in the first year. General system components comprise 17.4% of the total costs, and the cost items assigned to the TNA-RTW account for 32.4%. In contrast, the TNA workstation is responsible for only 7.4% of the total costs in the first year.

The total costs for one-time and annual material costs as well as annual personnel costs are summarized in Table 4.10. The total costs in the first year amount to 1,468,483 €, of which 9.7% are attributable to annual depreciation of one-time material costs, 48.7% to annual material costs, and 41.5% to annual personnel costs for operating the TNA system. Overall, total costs increase by approximately 1.2% per year, which is solely due to the calculated 3% annual increase in personnel costs.

If the annual total costs are allocated to the number of RTWs equipped with TNA technology, the first year under review results in 244,747 € per RTW. This value increases slightly over the years due to rising personnel costs.

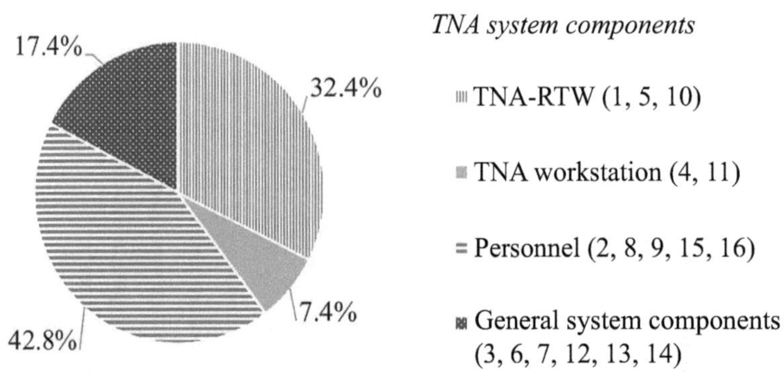


**Fig. 4.11** Distribution of costs by system components in the first year (Project Land|Rettung). *Source* Own illustration

**Table 4.10** Average total costs (Project Land|Rettung). *Source* Own illustration

| | Average annual costs [€] | | |
|---|---|---|---|
| | Year 1 | Year 2 | Year 3 |
| One-time material costs | 143,044 | 143,044 | 143,044 |
| Annual material costs | 715,869 | 715,869 | 715,869 |
| Annual personnel costs | 609,571 | 627,858 | 646,694 |
| total costs | 1,468,483 | 1,486,770 | 1,505,606 |

## 4.2.2 Standard Care

### 4.2.2.1 Relevant Structures

The following section provides a detailed description of the changes compared to the equipment presented in Sect. 4.2.1.1 as part of the project. Once again, the presentation is structured according to the core elements of the TNA system: TNA-RTW, TNA workstation, personnel, and general system components. Furthermore, the training design for all employees will fundamentally differ from the previous status quo after the end of the project, which is why training represents an additional core element of the TNA system in the context of the expansion to standard care described here.

Most of the changes can be assigned to the cost items already presented, as they replace the previous ones through restructuring. In these cases, the cost item number is supplemented with an “a”. All cost items from number 17 onward refer to system components that must be considered in addition to the status quo of the project measures (see Table 4.11).

*TNA-RTW*

In addition to equipping all 28 RTWs in the district with telemedical equipment for tele-emergency physician communication (1a), additional replacement vehicles (1b) must be provided to account for the possibility of an RTW being out of service. Six of the 28 RTWs have already been equipped as part of the Land|Rettung project. Currently, the emergency medical services maintain 10 replacement vehicles for the district, which corresponds to an additional 26% of the regularly operational RTWs. In the context of tele-emergency care as part of standard care, the 10 replacement vehicles will also be equipped with telemedical equipment. The conversion of a total of 32 RTWs in the district will incur both investment costs (1a and 1b) and material costs in the form of conversion costs (5a).

**Table 4.11** Structure of cost calculation by cost item for routine care in district V-G. *Source* Own illustration

| | Cost item | Definition |
|---|---|---|
| **One-time material costs** | | |
| 1a | Equipment per regular TNA-RTW | Costs for telemedicine equipment for regular RTWs |
| 1b | Equipment for TNA replacement RTW | Costs for telemedicine equipment for replacement RTWs |
| 4a | Redundant TNA work-station | Procurement and setup of redundant TNA workstation |
| 5a | Conversion of TNA-RTW | Installation of telemedicine equipment in an RTW |
| 17 | Uninterruptible power supply | Ensuring 24/7 routine TNA operations |
| 18 | TNA training | Design and preparation of in-district TNA training |
| **Annual material costs** | | |
| 10a | TNA-RTW | Technical operation of telemedicine equipment in TNA-RTWs, including support and maintenance |
| 11a | Tele-emergency doctor workstations | Technical operation of TNA workstations |
| 12a | Server infrastructure | Technical operation of network infrastructure/cloud (for 20–50 response units) |
| 13a | Third-party service technician | In case of system malfunctions/defects |
| 14a | Quality management system | Operator's flat fee |
| 19 | Peeq®BOX | Leasing costs |
| 20 | Training costs | Internal and external training and continuing educa-tion for all staff |
| **Annual personnel costs** | | |
| 15a | Medical service | Tele-emergency doctor and supervisor |
| 16a | Administration | Coordination and responsibility in the administrative area |

Since the peeq®BOX is the central unit that enables communication between on-site medical personnel and the tele-emergency doctor, two additional peeq®BOXes will be leased (19) to ensure standard care in the event of a failure.

In addition, an uninterruptible power supply (17) will secure standard care in the future. Annual operating costs (10a) are incurred for the operation of the 28 standard care RTWs. In the event a replacement RTW is used, the peeq®BOX is transferred, so no additional operating costs are incurred in this case.

*Tele-emergency doctor workstation*

A second, so-called redundancy workstation for the tele-emergency doctor (4a) ensures continuous (24/7) standard operation of the tele-emergency physician. This workstation is used if the primary workstation cannot be used for technical reasons. It also serves for training new tele-emergency physicians. Annual operating costs are incurred for the permanent use and operational readiness of both workstations (11a).

*General system components*

For the standard operation of the tele-emergency doctor system, annual operating costs are generally incurred for the server infrastructure (12a) and the quality management system (14a). In cases where additional services from third-party providers are used (e.g., in the event of system issues), flat-rate costs are incurred (13a). Based on previous experience in the project, it can be assumed that two independent working days of a service technician will be required annually.

*Personnel*

Personnel resources are budgeted to the same extent as in the project phase (10a; 11a). However, as described in Sect. 3.3.2.1, the calculation of annual personnel costs for the expansion to routine care differs from the previous approach.

*Training costs*

Initial staff training is no longer carried out exclusively by the third-party provider when the system is expanded. The effect of trained multipliers and the supervisor forms the basis for future training throughout the district. Some training sessions are conducted by a supervisor, and the associated opportunity costs due to lost working time must be considered individually.

For the initial design and preparation of a teleemergency doctor training (18), one-time material costs arise in the form of staff provided by University Medicine Greifswald for the duration of an average working month of the supervisor. All further training costs (20) are detailed below by occupational group. Table 4.12 summarizes the facts in tabular form.

**Table 4.12** Cost items for training under standard care in the V-G district. *Source* Own representation

| cost item | | Professional group (salary group) | Duration per person [in hours] | Number of participants |
|---|---|---|---|---|
| **TNA (prospectively 2 trainings per year)** | | | | |
| Within district | Working time for the duration of the training | TNA | 40 | 2 |
| | Instructor's working time | Senior physician | 40 | 1 |
| | Preparation time per training | Senior physician | 6 | 1 |
| | Training support by 2 paramedics (2 days each) | paramedic | 16 | 2 |
| | Flat rate for training materials per session | None | – | – |
| | One-time preparation (1/2 month) | Senior physician | 147 | 1 |
| **Station** | | | | |
| Within district | Working time for the duration of the training (1 training with 10 participants) | paramedic | 0* | – |
| | Instructor's working time | Senior physician | 8 | 1 |
| | Preparation time per training | Senior physician | 8 | 1 |
| **Supervisor** | | | | |
| Provider | Calculated training costs from the project** | None | 40 | 1 |
| | Working time for the duration of the training | TNA | 40 | 1 |
| | Flat-rate accommodation costs | None | | 1 |
| | Flat-rate travel expenses | None | | 1 |
| Within district | Working time for the duration of the training | TNA | 80 | 1 |
| | Instructor's working time | Senior physician | 80 | 1 |

(continued)

**Table 4.12** (continued)

| cost item | | Professional group (salary group) | Duration per person [in hours] | Number of participants |
|---|---|---|---|---|
| **Multiplier** | | | | |
| Internal to the district | Working hours for the duration of the training (12-person course) | paramedic | 8 | 12 |
| | Instructor's working hours | Senior physician | 8 | 1 |
| Provider | Imputed training costs from the project** (12-person course) | None | 8 | 12 |
| Internal to the district | 4 quarterly meetings per year (1 day each) | paramedic | 32 | All |
| | Working hours for the duration of the quarterly meeting | paramedic | 16 | All |
| | Working hours of the head of the quarterly meeting | Senior physician | 16 | 1 |

* covered in the annual training plan
** see Sect. 3.3.2.1

**Tele-emergency doctors**
Each year (taking into account staff turnover), two tele-emergency doctor training sessions are held, with two tele-emergency doctors trained per session. Each session lasts five days, with eight working hours per day. In addition, two paramedics are involved for two days each for practical exercises with the telemedicine equipment in the RTW. The training of the tele-emergency doctors is conducted by a supervisor.

The total training costs consist of the opportunity costs due to lost working time of the paramedics, the staff provided by University Medicine Greifswald (supervisor and teleemergency doctor), as well as the costs for training materials.

**Control center dispatchers**
The training of control center dispatchers was already carried out as part of the project. In view of staff turnover, multiplier effects apply, so that no further costs need to be budgeted.

**Ambulance station staff**

For the transition of the tele-emergency doctor system to routine operation, it is particularly necessary to train ambulance station staff in the use of teleemergency equipment. The training is provided as part of the regular annual continuing education days for ambulance station staff, so that no opportunity costs arise from lost working time.

A training session lasts one day (eight working hours), with up to ten employees able to participate simultaneously. Costs are incurred for the training day itself as well as for one day of preparation, covering the personnel costs for the supervisor provided by University Medicine Greifswald. Personnel changes due to staff turnover are managed by the multipliers and do not result in additional costs.

The majority of employees in the northern district have already been trained during the project period. One training session is still required for each of two stations. For three additional stations, a total of seven further training sessions are needed. In the southern district, a total of eleven training sessions are necessary to train all 110 employees for the first time. In total, 20 training sessions are required.

**Multipliers**

As part of the project, ten paramedics have so far been trained as multipliers. In the long term, two to three multipliers will be required at each of the 21 ambulance stations in the district. To reach the necessary minimum of 42 multipliers, three training sessions for multipliers (with a group size of twelve participants) will be held in 2020. Personnel changes due to staff turnover will be covered by the work of the multipliers and will not incur any additional costs from 2021 onwards.

The multiplier training consists of one training day with an external provider and one day of internal district training with a supervisor (each comprising eight working hours). The costs for the training day with the external provider already include travel to and from the training site for the instructor. These costs comprise the external provider's fee, the personnel costs for staff provided by University Medicine Greifswald, and the opportunity costs of the paramedics' working hours during training.

In addition, annual quarterly meetings for multipliers are planned as continuing education. Preparation and implementation of the training each require one day (eight working hours each) and are led by the supervisor. The opportunity costs of the participating multipliers' working hours are also taken into account. An average participation rate of 66% of the trained multipliers is assumed. Thus, in 2020, 26 participants (=10+36=46*2/3*10/12) and in 2021, 31 participants (=46*2/3) are expected.

**Supervisor**

To date, one supervisor has been trained. In the future, a second supervisor is to be trained. Supervisor training consists of one week with an external provider on site and two weeks of internal district training with the already trained supervisor.

The costs include one week of training with the external provider, plus travel and accommodation.[2] In addition, for the duration of the training, personnel costs are incurred for both the trainer and the trainee provided by University Medicine Greifswald.

#### 4.2.2.2 Individual Costs and Average Total Costs

Table 4.14 presents the individual cost items for the fourth and fifth years of analysis. These include, on the one hand, the cost items described in the previous chapter for an expansion into routine care, and on the other hand, those cost items for which depreciation of investments continues into the fourth and fifth years. The latter are indicated by the entry "depreciation amount" in the column (gross unit price).

Among the one-time investments, the costs for equipping all 28 regular operation ambulances and the ten replacement ambulances amount to € 719,712 (= € 22,491 · 32 advanced life support ambulances), and the depreciation of the first six equipped ambulances totals € 768,376, representing the highest cost items. The next highest cost item is the additional material costs for retrofitting the ambulances, at € 193,440 (= € 6045 · 32 advanced life support ambulances). All other listed cost items are comparatively low, at up to € 21,116. Taking annual depreciation into account, these two cost items also stand out as the largest. It is also evident that almost all cost items remain the same over the two years. Only items 8 and 9 incur no costs in the fifth year, as the defined depreciation period of four years has already ended. All other cost items resulting from depreciation of material costs in the first year end in the fifth year. In the future, new acquisitions are to be expected here, unless these goods are replaced by other cost items from the fourth year onwards. Since the completed depreciation costs in the fifth year relate to training and, as previously described, the training structure has been completely revised, there is no need for new investment.

[2] For five working days, six overnight stays are assumed in order to ensure eight-hour workdays.

Among the annual costs, the operator's flat fee for all 28 regular operation ambulances is the highest, at € 703,724, compared to other annual cost items. Personnel costs for the medical service are also high, at € 631,002. In addition, operation of the TNA workstation and the redundancy workstation incurs annual costs of € 118,594.

Training costs in the first year of analysis are still € 103,440. However, these costs are halved in the following year, as the restructuring of the training concept is expected to generate multiplier effects (see Sect. 4.2.2).

To provide an overview of which system components need to be particularly expanded when scaling the system to routine care, the costs are broken down by the core elements of the TNA system at this point, as already done in Sect. 4.2.1.2 (see Fig. 4.12).

The numbers in parentheses here also indicate the allocation of individual cost items. In the standard care scenario, the share of costs for the TNA workstation and redundancy workstation in the fourth year of analysis is 6.4%, which is 1% lower than in the first year. Personnel costs account for the largest share at 42.4%, similar to the first year of analysis. In contrast, the costs for general system components decrease to less than one third (from 17.4% to 4.9%), while the costs for the equipment and operational readiness of all TNA ambulances in the district rise to 46.3%. In comparison, these costs were only 32.4% in the first year.

The total costs in the fourth year of analysis amount to € 2,063,601, and in the fifth year to € 1961,280 (see

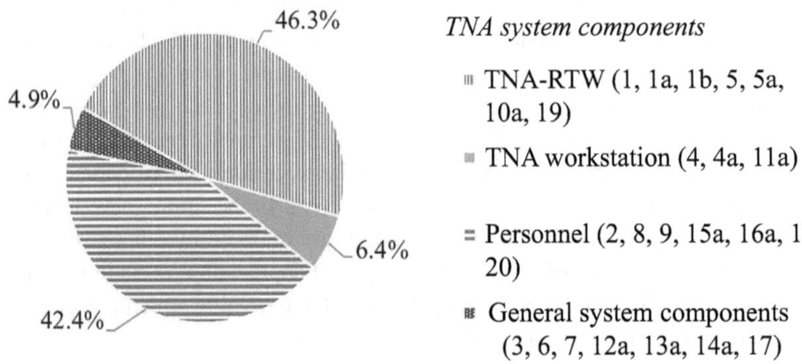


**Fig. 4.12** Distribution of costs by system components in the 4th year under routine care. *Source* Own illustration

**Table 4.13** Average total costs of standard care. *Source* Own representation

| | Average costs [€] | |
|---|---|---|
| | 4th year | 5th year |
| One-time material costs | 355,636 | 287,164 |
| Annual material costs | 1,013,563 | 958,300 |
| Annual personnel costs | 694,402 | 715,816 |
| Total costs | 2,063,601 | 1,961,280 |

Table 4.13). There is a slight decrease in costs from the fourth to the fifth year in the area of one-time and annual material costs, as well as a slight increase in annual personnel costs.

### 4.2.3 Standard Cost Function

With knowledge of all relevant cost types and amounts from Sects. 4.2.1.1 and 4.2.2.1, it is now possible to specify the standard cost function developed in Sect. 3.3.2.2. The cost function, which is presented again here, previously depended on various variables that have now been reviewed for relevance.

$$K\left(a; p^i; x; s_i\right) = C_I(a) + C_{II}\left(p^i\right) + C_{III}(x; a) + C_{IV}(s_i) + C_V(x) \quad (4.1)$$

The following section describes how the cost items from Table 4.14 were assigned to the respective cost groups. The numbering of the cost items from Sect. 4.2.2.2 is used again here.

The *one-time material costs* $C_I$ of the TNA system include the procurement of training materials (8) as well as software for the training of tele-emergency physicians (2) (e.g., a monitor patient box for training purposes, which transmits vital data to the tele-emergency physician during deployment), as well as the acquisition, setup, and integration of a network infrastructure (3; 7). One-time material costs also arise from setting up the TNA workstation (4) and a redundancy workstation (4a), which is needed, for example, in the event of technical failures at the primary workstation or for training purposes.

The quality management system also incurs one-time costs that must be taken into account (6). The uninterruptible power supply (17) is also considered a one-time material cost for the TNA workstation, as it ensures telecommunications in the event of network issues. Finally, the one-time costs for designing the TNA training courses (18) are also included in the one-time material costs, as these are only incurred at the initial implementation of a TNA system.

**Table 4.14** Breakdown of individual costs in standard care. *Source* Own representation

| | Cost item | *4th year* | | | *5th year* | | |
|---|---|---|---|---|---|---|---|
| | | Unit price Gross [€] | Quantity | Total price Gross [€] | Unit price Gross [€] | Quantity | Total price Gross [€] |
| **One-time material costs** | | | | | | | |
| 1 | Equipment per ambulance | *Depreciation* | | 48,664 | *Depreciation* | | 48,664 |
| 1a | Equipment per ambulance | 22,491 | 22 | 98,960 | | | 98,960 |
| 1b | Equipment per replacement ambulance | 22,491 | 10 | 44,982 | | | 44,982 |
| 2 | TNA training software | *Depreciation* | | 5428 | *Depreciation* | | 5428 |
| 3 | Network infrastructure | *Depreciation* | | 9416 | *Depreciation* | | 9416 |
| 4 | TNA workstation | *Depreciation* | | 9766 | *Depreciation* | | 9766 |
| 4a | Redundancy workstation | 23,749 | 1 | 4750 | | | 4750 |
| 5 | Conversion TNA-ambulance | *Depreciation* | | 7254 | *Depreciation* | | 7254 |
| 5a | Conversion TNA-ambulance | 6,045 | 32 | 38,688 | | | 38,688 |
| 6 | Quality management system | *Depreciation* | | 3904 | *Depreciation* | | 3904 |
| 7 | Network setup | *Depreciation* | | 7221 | *Depreciation* | | 7221 |
| 8 | Training materials | *Depreciation* | | 139 | | | 0 |
| 9 | Training costs | *Depreciation* | | 68,333 | | | 0 |
| 17 | Uninterruptible power supply | 17,850 | 1 | 5950 | | | 5950 |
| 18 | TNA training | 10,827 | 1 | 2707 | | | 2707 |

(continued)

**Table 4.14** (continued)

| | Cost item | *4th year* | | | *5th year* | | |
|---|---|---|---|---|---|---|---|
| | | Unit price Gross [€] | Quantity | Total price Gross [€] | Unit price Gross [€] | Quantity | Total price Gross [€] |
| **Annual operating costs** | | | | | | | |
| 10a | TNA-ambulance | 25,133 | 28 | 703,724 | 25,133 | 28 | 703,718 |
| 11a | Teleemergency doctor workstations | | | 118,594 | | | 118,594 |
| | License (primary) | 71,876 | 1 | 71,876 | 71,876 | 1 | 71,876 |
| | License (redundancy) | 7188 | 1 | 7188 | 7188 | 1 | 7188 |
| | Training license | 25,130 | 1 | 25,130 | 25,130 | 1 | 25,130 |
| | Facility rental | 7200 | 2 | 14,400 | 7200 | 2 | 14,400 |
| 12a | Server infrastructure | 51,690 | | 51,690 | 51,690 | | 51,690 |
| 13a | Provider service technician | 1607 | 2 | 3214 | 1607 | 2 | 3214 |
| 14a | Quality management | 19,992 | 1 | 19,992 | 19,992 | 1 | 19,992 |
| 19 | Peeq®BOX leasing | 6455 | 2 | 12,909 | 6455 | 2 | 12,909 |
| | Cost item | 4th year | | | 5th year | | |
| | | Unit price Gross [€] | Quantity | Total price Gross [€] | Unit price Gross [€] | Quantity | Total price Gross [€] |
| 20 | Training sessions | | | 103,440 | | | 48,183 |
| | Tele-emergency doctor | 8993 | 2 | 17,986 | 9254 | 2 | 18,508 |
| | Quarterly meetings multipliers | 948 | 26 | 24,652 | 957 | 31 | 29,675 |

(continued)

**Table 4.14** (continued)

| | Cost item | *4th year* | | | *5th year* | | |
|---|---|---|---|---|---|---|---|
| | | Unit price Gross [€] | Quantity | Total price Gross [€] | Unit price Gross [€] | Quantity | Total price Gross [€] |
| | multipliers | 6075 | 3 | 18,225 | | 0 | 0 |
| | Rescue station | 1180 | 20 | 23,600 | | 0 | 0 |
| | Supervisory staff | 18,977 | 1 | 18,977 | | 0 | 0 |
| **Annual personnel costs** | | | | | | | |
| 15a | Medical service | 232,841 | 5.5 | 631,002 | 239,827 | 5.5 | 649,932 |
| 16a | Administration | 63,400 | 1 | 63,400 | 65,884 | 1 | 65,884 |

The costs of the aforementioned items are each divided by the legally prescribed depreciation period in Table 3.3 and then summed.

Within the project, the training of other staff groups was carried out by the TNA system service provider. In the future, it is expected that these trainings could also be conducted internally. Since several staff groups are involved, but the training is less complex compared to that of the tele-emergency physician, it is assumed that, on average, one working month will also be required to design the training for each additional staff group.

The *annual personnel costs* $C_{II}$ include cost items 15a for the medical service and 16a for administration. These costs must be summed, taking into account the actual number of full-time equivalent positions required.

The *annual operating costs* $C_{III}$ comprise the annual costs for the use of the TNA workstation (11a), which include the costs for licenses, workstations, and rental of premises as well as the use of training software. License costs are determined by the number of active TNA workstations, as is the rent for the premises of the TNA center. In addition, the annual operating costs also include costs for the server infrastructure (12a), service provider services (13), quality management costs (14a), and the leasing of Peeq®BOXes (19). Furthermore, annual costs for operating the TNA-RTW (10a) are incurred, which are also included in the annual operating costs. For the district of V-G, calculations for standard care were based on leasing two Peeq®BOXes. In practice, the number will likely be adjusted to the structural conditions of the region under consideration and will therefore ultimately depend on the number of ambulances to be retrofitted.

The *variable training costs* $C_{IV}$ represent intangible investments in staff training and depend on the number of individuals to be trained in each staff group. The costs are allocated over four years. Section 4.2.2.2 presents the costs per training session. In order to develop a generally applicable standard cost function, the costs per training participant must be defined so that the annual number of individuals to be trained in a staff group ($s_i$) can be included as a variable in the cost function. For this purpose, the costs per training group were divided by the number of participants. This yields average training costs per person ($\gamma_i$), which are then multiplied by the corresponding variable $s_i$.

$$\sum_{i=1}^{5} \gamma_i \cdot s_i \tag{4.2}$$

with

| i | Group of persons |
|---|---|
| 1 | TNA |
| 2 | Multiplier |
| 3 | Rescue station staff |
| 4 | Supervisor |
| 5 | Integrated control center |

*The costs of RTW equipment* $C_V$ imply one-time material costs incurred for equipping the RTW with the necessary technical equipment (1; 1a; 1b) as well as costs for the conversion of TNA-capable RTW (5; 5a). These costs are directly dependent on the number of RTW to be retrofitted (x). The cost per RTW differs, amounting to € 40,554 (project) compared to € 22,491 (regular operation). For further analyses, the costs for regular operation are used as a basis.

Although the retrofitting of replacement TNA-RTW and regular operation TNA-RTW incurs costs of the same amount, the variable for regular operation RTW already serves as the sole variable for regular operation RTW in the calculation of annual operating costs. Therefore, the variable x is specified at this point. The total number of RTW (x) is thus composed of the sum of replacement TNA-RTW ($x^E$) and regular operation TNA-RTW ($x^R$). This adjustment is also applied to the annual operating costs.

Based on all relevant costs and their amounts from Tables 4.9 and 4.14, the following partial functions can be established:

$$C_I(a; a_r) = 178{,}828 + 48{,}831 \cdot a + 23{,}749 \cdot a_r \tag{4.3}$$

$$C_{II}\left(p^{TNA}; p^V\right) = 232{,}841 \cdot p^{TNA} + 63{,}400 \cdot p^V \tag{4.4}$$

$$\begin{aligned} C_{III}(a; a_r; x) = {} & 87{,}805 + 78{,}076 \cdot a + 39{,}518 \cdot a_r \\ & + 25{,}133 \cdot x^R \end{aligned} \tag{4.5}$$

$$\begin{aligned} C_{III}\left(s^{TNA}; s^M; s^{RW}; s^S; s^L\right) = {} & 4497 \cdot s^{TNA} + 506 \cdot s^M + 118 \cdot s^{RW} \\ & + 18{,}977 \cdot s^S + 2222 \cdot s^L \end{aligned} \tag{4.6}$$

$$C_V(x) = 28{,}536 \cdot \left(x^R + x^E\right) \tag{4.7}$$

with

| | |
|---|---|
| $a$ | Number of TNA workstations |
| $a_r$ | Number of TNA redundancy workstations |
| $p^{TNA}$ | Number of TNA full-time positions |
| $p^V$ | Number of administrative full-time positions |
| $s^M$ | Number of multipliers to be trained |
| $s^L$ | Number of control centers to be trained |
| $s^{RW}$ | Number of ambulance station staff to be trained |
| $s^S$ | Number of supervisory staff to be trained |
| $s^{TNA}$ | Number of tele-emergency physicians to be trained |
| $x^R$ | Number of regular-operation TNA ambulances |
| $x^E$ | Number of replacement TNA ambulances |

This yields a total cost function that indicates the average annual total costs of the TNA system. The cost levels refer to the year 2020.

$$\begin{aligned} K = 178828{+}48831 \cdot a + 23749 \cdot a_r + 232841 \cdot p^{TNA} + 63400 \cdot p^V + 87805 \\ + 78076 \cdot a + 39518 \cdot a_r + 25133 \cdot x^R + 4497 \cdot s^{TNA} + 506 \cdot s^M \\ + 118 \cdot s^{RW} + 18977 \cdot s^S + 2222 \cdot s^L + 28536 \cdot \left(x^R + x^E\right) \end{aligned} \tag{4.8}$$

Since the factors with the variables a, $a_r$ and x appear multiple times, these terms can be combined, as can the fixed costs that are not related to variables.

$$\begin{aligned} K = 266633{+}126907 \cdot a + 63267 \cdot a_r + 232841 \cdot p^{TNA} + 63400 \cdot p^V \\ + 53669 \cdot x^R + 4497 \cdot s^{TNA} + 506 \cdot s^M + 118 \cdot s^{RW} + 18977 \cdot s^S \\ + 2222 \cdot s^L \end{aligned} \tag{4.9}$$

With knowledge of the variable values, the formula can be used to calculate the average total costs K for the implementation of a TNA system.

## 4.3 Centralization Versus Decentralization

The results are presented based on the research questions defined in Sect. 3.4.[3]

*(1) What is the probability that an incoming call cannot be answered and thus enters a kind of waiting queue?*

In the post-observation period, 3019 cases were managed by the tele-emergency physician. This corresponded to an average of 4.32 cases per day. In 253 emergencies, the TNA was engaged for only one minute or less, which was not representative compared to the rest of the cases. Therefore, these cases were excluded from the analysis. Additionally, three cases that each lasted longer than three hours were also excluded. The final number of cases considered was thus 2763, resulting in an average of 3.94 cases per day. The minimum duration was 63 seconds and the maximum duration was 03:32:19 hours. On average, a case lasted 1477 seconds (00:24:37) with a standard deviation of 928 seconds. As already described in Sect. 4.1.4.1, a large number of calls to the tele-emergency physician were received between 8:00 a.m. and 1:00 p.m. compared to all other times of day, with a peak between 10:00 a.m. and 11:00 a.m. Only a few parallel cases were handled by the TNA. In principle, as previously described, there is no technical limit to the number of parallel cases. However, the tele-emergency physicians surveyed as part of the project indicated that managing two parallel emergencies is generally feasible.

Considering the entire day, the arrival rate $\lambda$ was 0.18, and during peak times it was 0.27. For the service rate $\mu$, the data indicated a throughput of 2.57. As shown in Sect. 3.4, the negative exponential distribution should theoretically be suitable for the service process, which was confirmed in the publication by Fleßa et al.[4] For the queueing model of the form M/M/2*m; $\infty$; FIFO, the peak load of incoming calls was decisive. It was further assumed that the service time is independent of the arrival time of the cases. The probability that a call could not be answered because the tele-emergency physician was already occupied with two parallel cases was 0.03%. This situation was subsequently defined as system overload. A significant increase in the arrival rate did not make a substantial difference. To reach a waiting rate of 10%, the arrival rate would have to be 2.093, which is 7.7 times higher than the empirical data from this district.

[3] Based on the publication by Fleßa et al (2021) „Telemedical emergency services: central or decentral coordination?“

[4] See Fleßa et al. (2021), p. 6.

*(2) How many emergency physicians would need to work in parallel in a TNA center, and how many regions (e.g., districts) could then be covered together? (Assumption: consistent quality and safety of care compared to the decentralized model.)*

The analysis was based on the assumption that all regions (e.g., districts) have the same arrival distribution and service rate, regardless of the degree of centralization. Furthermore, it was assumed that there were six TNA ambulances, as in the model region. Figure 4.13 shows the probability calculations for a call having to wait because the emergency physician is already engaged (depending on the number of TNAs working in parallel). The probability of system overload increases with the number of ambulances.

If two regions are considered, assuming the same structural characteristics as district V-G, the probability of system overload increases to 0.22%. In this case, 12 ambulances would be managed by one TNA. The overload probability rises to 19.81% with 60 ambulances (10 regions). A 100% overload probability would only be reached with 114 ambulances (19 regions) if only one TNA is responsible for managing emergencies. In this scenario, it would be certain that not all incoming emergency calls could be handled by the TNA, as they would already

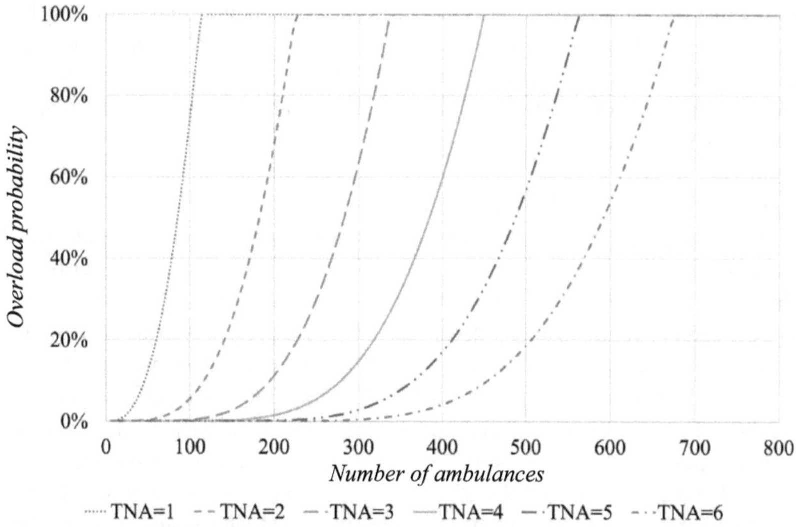


**Fig. 4.13** Probability of overload depending on the number of ambulances and TNAs. *Source* Own illustration based on Fleßa et al. (2021), p. 7

be engaged in two parallel cases. Expanding the TNA system to include additional tele-emergency physicians would reduce the probability of overload for the respective number of ambulances covered. Two tele-emergency physicians could thus manage up to 228 ambulances, but almost all emergency calls would have to wait and could not be immediately handled by the TNA. Looking at the other curves in the figure, it becomes clear that the number of tele-emergency physicians has a significant impact on the probability of overload.

Further analysis examined how the number of required TNAs develops depending on a maximum probability of overload. Figure 4.14 presents the results for maximum overload probabilities of 1%, 5%, 10%, and 20%. With a maximum probability of a call not being answered of 20%, a single tele-emergency physician could manage 60 ambulances, corresponding to 10 regions. With two TNAs, 138 ambulances could be managed; with three TNAs, 222 ambulances; with four TNAs, 408 ambulances; and with five TNAs, 504 ambulances could be managed without exceeding the maximum overload probability. The figure also illustrates a variety of scenarios. For example, if 186 ambulances (corresponding to 31 regions) were to be managed by the tele-emergency physician, and the probability of overload should not exceed 10%, four TNAs would be required to provide tele-emergency services.

Table 4.15 once again presents the respective maximum values (number of ambulances or regions to be supervised) for the defined maximum overload probabilities of 1%, 5%, 10%, and 20%. For example, if 186 ambulances (corresponding to 31 regions) are to be supervised by the TNA, with the probability of overload not exceeding 10%, four tele-emergency physicians would be required to cover the tele-emergency medical service.

*(3) Does the centralized TNA service offer cost advantages?*

To address this question, the relevant cost components first had to be identified. The results were based on the cost structure of a TNA system as described by Prasser et al. (2020). As already outlined in Sect. 3.4, only those costs that differ between the centralized and decentralized alternatives were considered. When focusing on the costs of a TNA system per TNA office, fixed, step-fixed, and variable cost characteristics can be identified. The variable costs per emergency do not differ between the centralized and decentralized alternatives and were therefore disregarded in the analysis. Table 4.16 presents the relevant cost components.

The fixed costs $C_f$ of a TNA office were independent of the number of emergency calls received and the number of tele-emergency physicians on duty. Thus, only the cost items for rent of the TNA central office premises, support and maintenance, the mandatory quality management system, and personnel costs for

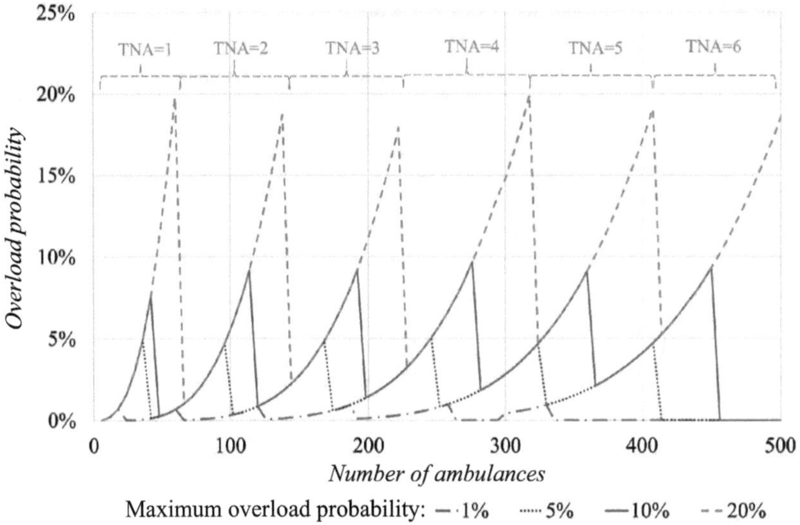


**Fig. 4.14** Probability of overload at different maximum probabilities. *Source* Own illustration based on Fleßa et al. (2021), p. 8[5]

supervision and administration needed to be considered. In principle, these costs could increase if a critical number of tele-emergency physicians working in parallel were reached. However, in the present model it was assumed that this number would not be reached under realistic conditions, and the costs would therefore remain constant.

The step-fixed costs *v* depended on the number of tele-emergency physicians working simultaneously in the offices. As shown in the table, personnel costs for the 24/7 operation of the telemedical service represented the largest cost item in the analysis. In addition, depreciation of workplace equipment and network infrastructure as well as license fees for the TNA workstation were relevant. It was assumed that these costs would increase as the number of TNAs working in an office increased. In total, the annual costs for a TNA office amounted to € 696,949.

[5] Note: The required number of TNAs is specified only for a maximum overload probability of 20%.

**Table 4.15** Number of ambulances as a function of the maximum overload probability. *Source* Own illustration based on Fleßa et al. (2021)

| | Max. number of advanced life support ambulances (or regions) | | | |
|---|---|---|---|---|
| Number of TNA | *at a maximum overload probability of* | | | |
| | *1%* | *5%* | *10%* | *20%* |
| **1** | 18 (3) | 36 (6) | 42 (7) | 60 (10) |
| **2** | 60 (10) | 96 (16) | 114 (19) | 138 (23) |
| **3** | 120 (20) | 162 (27) | 192 (32) | 222 (37) |
| **4** | 186 (31) | 240 (40) | 270 (45) | 318 (53) |
| **5** | 258 (43) | 324 (54) | 360 (60) | 408 (68) |
| **6** | 330 (55) | 408 (68) | 456 (76) | 504 (84) |

**Table 4.16** Annual costs for the TNA service. *Source* Own representation based on Fleßa et al. (2021)

| Cost type | cost item | Costs per year [€] | Total costs per year [€] |
|---|---|---|---|
| **Fixed**($C_f$) | Rent | 7,200 | **148,876** |
| | Support, maintenance | 3116 | |
| | Quality management system | 27,560 | |
| | Personnel costs for administration and supervision | 111,000 | |
| **Step-fixed**($v$) | Personnel costs TNA (24/7 operation) | 508,144 | **548,073** |
| | Training of TNA | 6924 | |
| | Network infrastructure | 20,797 | |
| | License for TNA workstation | 12,208 | |

Furthermore, the number of tele-emergency physicians working simultaneously in an office depended on the number of ambulances equipped for telemedicine that were being supported in a given region. In the district of V-G, six ambulances were equipped with telemedicine technology as part of the Land|Rettung project. For further analyses, it was always assumed that there were six TNA ambulances per region.

To determine the total costs incurred for the decentralized ($C_d$) and centralized ($C_z$) alternatives, a cost function was developed for each. It was assumed that the amounts of fixed and step-fixed costs were fundamentally identical and depended solely on the influencing variables, regardless of the alternative selected. The decentralized total costs $C_d$ are the sum of fixed and step-fixed costs, depending on the number of TNA offices (or regions).

$$C_d = n \cdot (C_f + v) \tag{4.10}$$

$$= n \cdot 696{,}949 \tag{4.11}$$

In contrast, the centralized TNA office, which serves multiple regions, depends on the number of tele-emergency physicians working in the office. The total costs of the centralized alternative $C_z$ are given by the cost function:

$$C_z = C_f + e \cdot v \tag{4.12}$$

$$= 148{,}876 + e \cdot 548{,}073 \tag{4.13}$$

With

| | |
|---|---|
| $C_d$ | Total costs of the decentralized alternative for n regions |
| $C_z$ | Total costs of the centralized alternative for n regions |
| $n$ | Number of regions |
| $C_f$ | Fixed costs for establishing a TNA office |
| $v$ | Step-fixed costs for operating a TNA office |
| $e$ | Number of TNA working in parallel in one office, e = f(n) |

Figure 4.15 shows the unit cost functions as a function of the number of regions considered for the alternatives of a decentralized and a centralized TNA system. It should be noted that, in the case of decentralized coordination, the unit costs must be multiplied by the number of regions independently operating the telemedicine service. The maximum overload probability in this representation is 5%. The curve "Decentralized (6 of 26)" represents the status in the V-G district, with six retrofitted TNA ambulances. The curve "Decentralized (26 of 26)" shows the unit cost function when all ambulances in the region (in V-G, there are 26 ambulances) are supported by tele-emergency physicians. The function allows the costs per region to be determined depending on the number of regions. The "Centralized" line represents the costs incurred with centralized coordination of the telemedicine service, i.e., with a single TNA office. These amount to a constant annual cost of just under € 700,000. If each region operates its own TNA office, the average annual costs amount to € 696,949. When only one region is

considered, the costs for all three alternatives are the same. This is because a single tele-emergency physician can cover up to 36 ambulances without the probability of a call delay exceeding 5%. Thus, according to Table 4.16, the same costs for system readiness and usability arise in both alternatives. The figure also shows that unit costs decrease significantly as more regions are centralized.

For example, if 20 regions are considered, each maintaining 26 ambulances in operational readiness and the maximum overload probability must not exceed 5%, a total of six tele-emergency physicians are required in parallel to serve the regions (one TNA per region). The annual costs per region for decentralized coordination amount to approximately € 171,900, resulting in a total of € 3,438,000 for all 20 regions. In comparison, the centralized tele-emergency service incurs costs of € 696,949. Thus, in this case, the centralized TNA system is only about one fifth as expensive as the decentralized alternative.

Figure 4.15 shows the unit cost functions as a function of the number of regions considered for the alternatives of a decentralized and a centralized TNA system. It should be noted that, in the case of decentralized coordination, the unit costs must be multiplied by the number of regions independently operating the telemedicine service. The maximum overload probability in this representation is 5%. The curve "Decentralized (6 of 26)" represents the status in the V-G district, with six retrofitted TNA ambulances. The curve "Decentralized (26 of 26)" shows

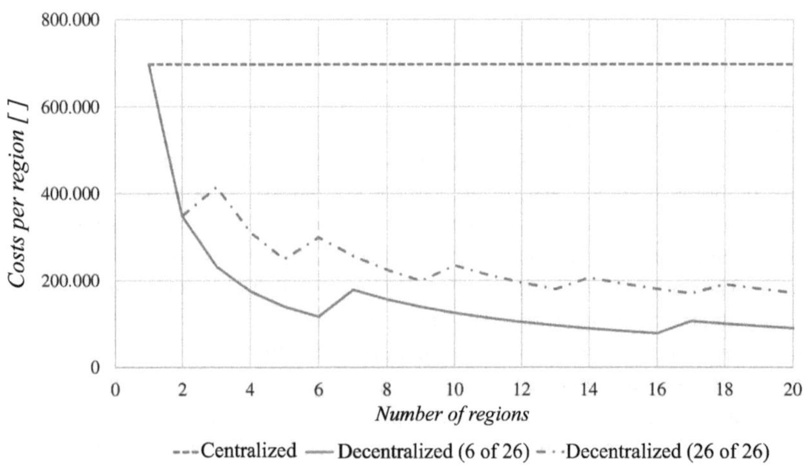


**Fig. 4.15** Cost function for centralization versus decentralization. *Source* Own illustration based on Fleßa et al. (2021), p. 8

the unit cost function when all ambulances in the region (in V-G, there are 26 ambulances) are supported by tele-emergency physicians. The function allows the determination of costs per region depending on the number of regions. The line "Centralized" represents the costs incurred with centralized coordination of the telemedicine service, i.e., with a single TNA office. These amount to a constant annual cost of just under € 700,000. If each region operates its own TNA office, the average annual costs amount to € 696,949. When only one region is considered, the costs for all three alternatives are the same. This is because a single tele-emergency physician can supervise up to 36 ambulances without the probability of a delayed call exceeding 5%. Thus, according to Table 4.16, the same costs for system readiness and usability arise in both alternatives. The figure also shows that unit costs decrease significantly as more regions are centralized.

For example, if 20 regions are considered, each maintaining 26 ambulances in operational readiness and the maximum overload probability must not exceed 5%, a total of six tele-emergency physicians are required in parallel to serve the regions (one TNA per region). The annual costs per region for decentralized coordination amount to approximately € 171,900, resulting in a total of € 3,438,000 for all 20 regions. In comparison, the centralized tele-emergency service incurs costs of € 696,949. Thus, in this case, the centralized TNA system is only about one fifth as expensive as the decentralized alternative.

# 5 Discussion

## 5.1 Impacts on the Deployment Structure

The analysis of the deployment structure before and after the introduction of the TNA system clearly shows that several parameters have changed. The model region V-G is a popular Baltic Sea destination for many tourists, resulting in seasonal fluctuations in the number of deployments, especially during the summer months. A pre-post comparison revealed a decrease in the average number of NEF deployments, accompanied by a slight increase in the average number of RTW missions within the scope of primary emergency care. The increase in secondary mission numbers from the transition phase onward could not be explained by the data or structural adjustments in the district. In this regard, it is assumed that errors occurred during data transfer due to differently set filter settings during data export. Since the proportion of secondary missions in the district is comparatively low, it is currently difficult to make definitive statements about the impact of the TNA system. Furthermore, the TNA was responsible for only a relatively small number of secondary missions during the project period. The following discussion, based on the available results, will address the extent to which the deployment structure changed after the introduction of the TNA system and whether advantages in prehospital emergency care could be generated.

An overview of all deployments in the district showed that an average of 65.6 missions(pre) and 102.2 missions (post) per day took place. There were situations in which an emergency physician was occupied, while at the same time, another emergency call was received in the same region. If possible, the TNA can manage one of these missions together with the RTW paramedics, leaving the emergency physician available and ready for the more severe case. The number of TNA deployments fluctuated during the introduction phase and only stabilized



R. Süss, *The Tele-Emergency Physician System as an Innovation in Prehospital Emergency Care*, https://doi.org/10.1007/978-3-658-49561-9_5

in the defined post-phase from the second quarter of 2018 onward. Currently, an average of 402 telemedical missions take place per quarter. As the system is still relatively new and innovative in the model region, it is not yet possible to predict the future average number of tele-emergency physician missions per quarter. Furthermore, the deployment situation will depend on the number of RTWs affiliated with the TNA system. However, it is already evident that the number of NEF misisons has been influenced by the introduction of the TNA system. The trend of increasing missions for the emergency physician has been counteracted. The number of NEF deployments is overall declining. The participation rate of the conventional emergency physician in the entire district was 56.3% (pre) and 44.1% (post). A particularly marked decrease in NEF deployments was observed in the northern part of V-G, where the RTWs were equipped with telemedical technology. Here, the TNA took over approximately 18% of RTW deployments. These data clearly show that many missions can be managed by a tele-emergency physician and that the physical presence of an emergency physician is not necessary in every case. The medical evaluation results from the Land|Rettung project also show that the TNA managed patients of all age groups with varying degrees of injury and illness severity. Most patients treated by a TNA within the emergency rescue services were not in acute life-threatening situations.[1] For life-threatening cases, the physical presence of an emergency physician remains indispensable. The results suggest that the TNA is a valuable addition in terms of case severity between RTW deployments and those accompanied by an emergency physician.[2]

The average number of daily misisons for the NEF decreased from 42.9 (pre) to 38.4 (post). On average, this means 4.5 fewer deployments per day in which an NEF is co-dispatched. The analysis of tele-emergency physician mission data showed that a tele-emergency physician manages an average of 4.4 missions per day. The data thus demonstrate that the tele-emergency physician is able to adequately supplement and relieve patient care.

As part of the Land|Rettung project, patients were surveyed regarding their acceptance of and satisfaction with the system. The vast majority of patients agreed with the care provided by the TNA and found it pleasant. Only seven patients declined care during the study period.[3] The new form of care tested in the

[1] See Kuntosch et al. (2020), p. 161 ff.

[2] See Kuntosch et al. (2020), p. 162 f.

[3] See Kuntosch et al. (2020), p. 198 ff.

model region thus provides ideal conditions for adaptation into the existing emergency rescue services system, based on its acceptance. Since the TNA can only operate at the scene via telecommunication, it is entirely dependent on the cooperation of the emergency service staff. If, in particular, the RTW crew were not interested or intrinsically motivated to collaborate with the tele-emergency physician, the latter would have no means to fulfill their tasks and the system could not be implemented. Comprehensive and goal-oriented communication between both actors in this care model is essential for successful implementation, which is why acceptance among staff, alongside factors such as investment costs, infrastructure, and the decision-makers' openness to innovation, is crucial. Furthermore, patients must also agree to the new form of care provided by the TNA, as otherwise no treatment can take place. However, the results from the project show that acceptance is good to high on all sides and that the prerequisites have been established for the long-term and successful implementation of the TNA system.[4]

The analyses further showed that in over 72% of TNA missions, no emergency physician was co-dispatched. In only about 5% of deployments was an emergency physician additionally dispatched or requested at the start of the deployment. The development of mission activity in emergency rescue services across Germany is clearly reflected here—the incident frequency is not necessarily induced by the need for a physical emergency physician or even an emergency physician in general. In situations where a physical medical intervention by an emergency physician was not required, the TNA was able to de-escalate and relieve the situation by supporting the paramedics upon arrival of the RTW at the scene or by delegating tasks. In only 0.4% of all TNA deployments during the observation period was an NEF deployment taken over by a TNA. This also indicates that the tele-emergency physician within the TNA system is not intended as a stepwise replacement for the ground-based emergency physician, but rather to be deployed in non-life-threatening situations where the personnel resource of the emergency physician can be conserved for severe emergencies, such as cardiac arrest or polytrauma. Without communication with the TNA, the RTW crew is generally not permitted to decide on patient transport, which is why most patients are transported. Especially in minor cases that do not require inpatient treatment, patients are sometimes transported to the emergency department without necessity, gradually leading to the exhaustion or even overload of the system.[5] During

4 See Kuntosch et al. (2020), p. 212 ff.

5 See Kuntosch et al. (2020), p. 164.

the observation period, 23.8% of cases were managed on an outpatient basis by the TNA, so that in these cases no transport by RTW to an emergency department was necessary.[6] This demonstrates the potential of the TNA system not only in relieving the conventional emergency physician, but also with regard to clinical structures and the healthcare system as a whole.

The potential for purely telephone consultations or advisory discussions was also utilized by emergency resources that, during the project, were not yet equipped with telemedical devices and thus used only the telecommunication link to the tele-emergency physician. In the future, the proportion of such consultations could be further expanded. The tele-emergency physician has a clear advantage over the NEF emergency physician, as they are digitally networked and have extensive access to standard operating procedures. This enables them to access comprehensive information even during deployments, for example in rare case scenarios. This advantage can be made available to all emergency physicians in the district through brief communication. Paramedics can also seek reassurance by consulting the tele-emergency physician and obtain medical advice as needed, even if, for example, the involvement of an emergency physician is not strictly necessary according to the deployment description, since every emergency is unique and an incident timeline always involves a certain degree of uncertainty. It is fundamentally irrelevant whether the consultation is conducted by a telemedically equipped RTW or a conventional RTW. The continuous telephone availability of the tele-emergency physician offers all emergency service staff the opportunity for consultation. The results showed that this potential was also recognized and utilized by ambulance stations in the southern part of the district. Although the number of consultations by these non-telemedically equipped RTWs is still low, there is potential for expansion, reflecting the general interest and willingness of emergency service staff throughout the district to use the system.

The publication by Fleßa et al. (2016) demonstrated that, prior to the introduction of the TNA system, there were often rural regions that could not be reached within the legally defined response time limit. This limit ensures that the population always receives initial medical assistance within a specified time after notification of an emergency, and that transport to a medical facility is provided accordingly. Therefore, the impact of the TNA system on the response time limit should also be examined. However, the analysis results showed that the average response time limit for ambulances (RTW) increased from 9:49 ± 10:13 min to

[6] See Kuntosch et al. (2020), p. 164.

10:19 ± 17:37 min. The response time limit for emergency physician vehicles (NEF) increased by only a few seconds, reaching 10:36 ± 15:39 min in the post-implementation period. The median also changed very little in the pre-post comparison. Noteworthy is the large variance, which results from a high proportion of outliers with long to very long response times. Approximately 4% of the data sets were defined as outliers, which had a significant impact on the variance of the response time limit. Long response times of over 30 minutes are rare in the daily operations of prehospital emergency rescue services. It is conceivable that, during an operation, the status was not transmitted via the status button, so the arrival status received a later timestamp, resulting in data recording errors. Ultimately, such cases can only be verified individually by reviewing the operation protocol.

Thus, the TNA system appears to have little impact on the response time limit. However, it can be assumed that the TNA is also available upon the arrival of the RTW at the scene. The time difference to the actual response time limit of a TNA results only from establishing the telecommunication connection, which, in an emergency, should be reduced to just a few seconds. It would also be possible to establish telecommunication while the RTW is en route. Visual monitoring of the patient, however, can only take place once the patient is inside the RTW and thus within range of the camera installed in the vehicle. Overall, it can be assumed that the TNA is deployed more quickly in cases where the NEF has a longer travel distance than the RTW. This aspect, however, would need to be specifically investigated using response time calculations for the TNA in order to potentially obtain significant results and to examine the impact of the TNA system on the response time limit.

Misallocations continue to occur in prehospital emergency care. Such cases arise, for example, when there is no general medical need for treatment, a patient does not require transport, or the presence of an emergency physician is initially unclear and ultimately unnecessary. These cases tie up resources, especially personnel. In the interest of efficient allocation of scarce resources, misallocations should be avoided as much as possible, which is theoretically understandable but not so easy to implement in everyday emergency services. During the study period, the proportion of misallocations was 18.6% for RTW and around 10% for NEF. Here, it is the responsibility of the public and government to counteract the overburdening of emergency services and emergency departments. Further investigations in the Land|Rettung project showed that many Germans, for example, are not aware of the on-call medical service with the telephone number 116117. Broad communication about this option for timely medical care in non-life-threatening cases, without involving emergency rescue services, must be significantly expanded. In Sect. 4.1.4.2 the results on personnel binding times in the context of operations and misallocations were presented. It was shown that the proportion of misallocations among RTW operations remained apparently unaffected by the introduction of the TNA system. The proportion of misallocations for NEF decreased by about 1.2% and amounts to 10.2% of operations in the post-implementation period. An emergency physician is tied up in a false call for an average of 46 ± 34 min (see Table 4.7, Sect. 4.1.4.2). The involvement of an emergency physician in an operation for which they are not medically required for various reasons is therefore not negligible from an economic perspective, as travel and mission duration incur costs. In the post-implementation period, 2,636 emergency physician operations turned out to be false calls (see Table 4.1, Sect. 4.1.1). With an average binding time of 46 minutes, this corresponds to about 88 working hours of an emergency physician per month, plus the accompanying NEF crew personnel. By comparison, about 14% of TNA operations are classified as misallocations. In these cases, the TNA is only tied up for 4 ± 8 min. The significant difference in binding time is partly due to the elimination of travel time, which the emergency physician must cover even in the case of a misallocation. In the worst case, the NEF travels to a remote location, only to find on site that an emergency physician is not needed, so the NEF must return the entire way. In this respect, the TNA system offers further advantages, especially in rural areas where the distances between the scene and the base can be very great. On the other hand, it is also possible that an NEF is not initially dispatched, but it later turns out that a conventional emergency physician is needed after all. However, as the data showed, such cases were very rare. In such a case, the tele-emergency physician must bridge the operation as best as possible until the NEF arrives.

Furthermore, all parties involved in an operation have the option to terminate and subsequently re-establish the telemedical connection in an emergency, if necessary. The binding time of NEF emergency physician personnel would extend over the entire mission duration on site. The TNA, on the other hand, could potentially use the periods of "non-communication" efficiently to supervise another operation in parallel. The short binding time of the TNA thus proves advantageous for both operations and misallocations. Especially in cases where the actual need for physical medical assistance is questionable, it may be more efficient in terms of personnel deployment to consult the TNA rather than dispatch an emergency physician to the scene. The binding time of the emergency physician increased by an average of 3 minutes after system implementation, amounting to 63 ± 37 min in the post-implementation period. Since the introduction of the tele-emergency physician, the conventional emergency physician has thus been tied up in operations for a longer average duration. One possible explanation is that the tele-emergency physician was able to take over the less severe cases, allowing the emergency physician to be available for more serious operations, which generally involve longer mission durations. However, since the emergency physician overall accompanies fewer operations, this does not automatically result in an increase in the total binding time. Notably, the binding time of an RTW differs by 7 minutes depending on whether a TNA was involved in the operation or not. In addition to the general increase in binding time by 2 minutes (post $80 \pm 45$ min), an RTW with TNA is, according to the available mission data, tied up in an operation for a longer period. This may be related to the increased need for communication with the TNA, if the rescue or paramedic team at the scene receives information that can only be relayed to the TNA once in the RTW. However, since the results of the medical evaluation showed that the tele-emergency physician increasingly managed non-life-threatening situations, the question arises as to why the binding time with TNA is higher. To answer this, the individual operation processes would need to be examined in detail based on the operation protocols.

In the area of secondary missions, the average duration of engagement decreased by approximately 33 minutes in the pre-post comparison. Notably, an ambulance (RTW) is on average engaged for 140 minutes when accompanied by a TNA, but only 85 minutes when a conventional emergency physician is involved. Since there were only 63 TNA secondary missions during the entire post-period, these figures are relatively difficult to interpret. It is conceivable, however, that the TNA was deliberately assigned to longer missions in order to avoid overburdening emergency physicians and to create available capacity, thereby providing relief. The mission data do not indicate why the TNA has so far been rarely involved in this type of mission, even though they offer significant potential to conserve the resource of emergency physicians. Monitoring by the TNA, for example during a transfer, could result in an average time saving of 90 minutes for the conventional emergency physician, as the latter would not be available for other missions during this period. However, the proportion of secondary missions involving an emergency physician is small, so further analyses over a longer period are needed to make significant statements about the advantages of the TNA in secondary missions.

The integration of the TNA system carries the risk of interruptions in audio or visual communication, particularly in the case of poor network infrastructure. The system evaluation showed that there were repeated interruptions in communication during the observation period, both short-term and long-term. The outages ranged from a few minutes to several hours. These outages led to so-called "offline missions" for the tele-emergency physician, during which documentation in the software was either not possible or only possible to a limited extent. It is also conceivable that a brief communication failure could ultimately result in a longer deployment of the RTW, as emergency medical care for the patient would be temporarily interrupted and, for example, the emergency services personnel would not be authorized to act on instructions. This results in an increased engagement duration for the RTW or a deterioration in the quality of care in the event of a sudden but permanent failure of tele-emergency medical treatment. However, such extreme effects were not observed during the project period, as the audio connection was generally sufficient for operational purposes. In cases of persistent connection problems with the TNA, at least the audio connection could be restored via the mobile phone of the RTW crew or the patient, ensuring that emergency medical care could be maintained.[7]

With regard to the time of day of TNA missions, the data showed that especially between midnight and 6 a.m., hardly any missions were supported via telemedicine. Only about 13% of TNA missions took place during this period. The number of RTW missions during this time also accounted for just under 20% of all missions. It therefore appears that there are generally fewer emergency missions during this time span, which explains the similarly distributed number of TNA missions. Nevertheless, with almost 50 missions, the minimum number of missions over the post-period occurred between 4 and 5 a.m. During this time, there were also fewer parallel missions supervised by the TNA. This can be attributed on the one hand to the lower density of mission volume, but on the other hand, it could also be due to potentially more challenging working conditions (night shifts) at this hour. Tele-emergency physicians are free at any time to accept or decline a parallel mission, resulting in different hourly mission distributions depending on the TNA on duty.

The advantages of the TNA system in terms of efficient resource utilization are further confirmed by the results on consultation times. On average, a TNA is engaged in a mission for only 19 minutes, of which the active conversation with the RTW crew accounts for about 10 minutes of the total average mission duration. In the case of a false call, the TNA is engaged for an average of only 33 seconds, which offers clear advantages over an emergency physician who would also have to travel to the scene. However, it should be noted that the term "false call" must be distinguished between the conventional emergency physician and the TNA. Nevertheless, in cases where the emergency description at the dispatch center already suggests that the presence of an emergency physician is not required, the TNA offers clear time savings and thus cost advantages. In an aver-

[7] See Kuntosch et al. (2020), p. 166 f.

age RTW mission with an engagement of about 86 minutes, the TNA is actively involved in conversation for only 10 minutes. In a comparable case, the emergency physician would be engaged for more than six times as long on average. In addition, due to the short duration of conversations, the TNA could potentially supervise further cases in parallel, whereas the conventional emergency physician would be tied up in the same mission the entire time. Thus, the tele-emergency physician's service time can be used efficiently.

In summary, the results show that the deployment structure has changed since the introduction of the TNA system in the V-G model region. Although not all changes are yet significant and clearly measurable, they are already leading to a shift in the utilization of personnel resources. The mission duration of an emergency physician has increased, but at the same time, the number of missions for an emergency physician vehicle (NEF) has decreased. However, these results should by no means be interpreted as an indication for reducing the resource of emergency physicians, for example by closing emergency physician stations. The tele-emergency physician cannot replace the manual skills of an emergency physician at the patient's side. Rather, from a deployment statistics perspective, the TNA is an option to supplement and relieve the emergency rescue services. The system can generate available capacity to enable a long-term improvement in the quality of prehospital emergency care in the face of increasing challenges in this field.

## 5.2 Costs of the TNA System

In order to comprehensively evaluate the TNA system, the advantages resulting from the changes in deployment structure presented so far must be weighed against the costs. In Sect. 4.2 the costs were presented in detail and will be critically examined in the following chapter. As described in Sect. 2.4.3, the adoption of innovation depends on various factors. Only if the system is also financially viable will adoption of the model be possible. The following chapter discusses the costs of the system from the project perspective and in the context of scaling up to routine care.

It should first be noted that the costs of the system fundamentally depend on the provider. Many components and services were sourced from the same service provider. Choosing a different provider could potentially result in higher or lower prices for individual TNA system components, which would affect the total costs. At the start of the project, however, the provider was selected on the basis of a tendering process, which suggests at least a good price-performance ratio at project launch. Furthermore, this provider had already successfully implemented the system in the city of Aachen. In the long term, additional providers could enter the market and thus change prices by altering the supply and demand for telemedicine services.

A comparison of costs in both scenarios (project and routine care) reveals that there have been significant price reductions for many system components provided by the service provider. Figures 4.11 and 4.12 showed the percentage breakdown of costs by system component. The costs were divided into the categories TNA-RTW, TNA workstation, personnel, and general system components. A comparison of the two figures reveals clear changes in these four areas, which will be discussed in detail below.

The costs in the TNA-RTW category increased by 13.9% in the pre-post comparison. This change in total costs is due to the number of retrofitted RTWs. Although the unit price for equipping and retrofitting an RTW has halved, the multiplication of RTWs in the system has led to a significant increase in the share of this cost category. By equipping the remaining 22 regular RTWs and the ten backup RTWs kept in reserve, the number of RTWs to be equipped has increased more than fivefold, but the equipment and conversion were carried out in the same way as for the first six RTWs. The price reduction thus clearly represents a substantial volume discount from the service provider. If the TNA system were to be expanded to other regions, further discounts could be expected. However, it is not known whether, and to what extent, the service provider would grant such discounts.

The proportion of costs in the TNA workstation category has not changed. Based on the average low number of daily TNA deployments and the available deployment statistics, it can be assumed that providing coverage for the entire district with a single TNA workstation is feasible. Nevertheless, an additional workstation has been planned for the future, which will serve as a redundancy workstation. At a unit price of € 23,749, this is also significantly less expensive than the previously established TNA workstation (€ 47,082). The cost difference can be attributed to the type of workstation, as the redundancy workstation is not intended for continuous operation and will therefore differ in its equipment. The annual operating costs of the workstation are similar to those in the project status.

The proportion of personnel costs relative to the annual total costs of the TNA system has remained virtually unchanged at approximately 42.3%. Together with the costs for the TNA ambulances, these two categories account for nearly 89% of the total costs. Staff training in the project status was calculated based on the flat-rate total value for training provided by the service provider. It should be noted that personnel costs are always highly dependent on the federal state in question as well as individual collective agreements. The salary calculations used in this study can therefore only serve as a guideline. However, it can be assumed that the proportion of these costs compared to the other items in the TNA system would not fundamentally change as a result of salary adjustments. Only if the number of full-time positions—and thus the number of employed tele-emergency physicians—were increased would costs rise significantly. For example, if two tele-emergency physicians were to be on duty simultaneously, the number of full-time positions and thus the costs would have to double.

The costs for ongoing training in the event of an expansion to routine care were calculated based on Table 4.12. The duration of the training sessions was based on the training scope specified by the service provider for each professional group. The number of training hours per staff group was taken from the service provider's offer. The associated costs per training hour were distributed evenly across the total number of training sessions to be provided. It is conceivable that the service provider set different training costs for the individual staff groups. However, since this was not apparent from the offer, the costs were distributed evenly. For training in routine care, only the costs based on the project calculations for the supervision staff and the multipliers are included. The remaining training sessions are mostly conducted internally within the district and were calculated independently of the service provider's pricing.

The number of staff to be trained was calculated based on project experience, using staff turnover during the observation period as a guideline. Actual turnover may correspond to this assumption, but it could also develop differently. The scope of work in daily operations has changed for all affected staff in the emergency medical services and has been expanded to include the involvement of the tele-emergency physician. Depending on each employee's acceptance of the system, this may result in under- or over-challenging, and thus in motivation or demotivation. A fundamental attitude toward work ultimately influences the decision whether an employee changes workplace or remains. The results of the project evaluation showed that 71% of the 212 emergency medical service employees surveyed in the district considered the TNA system to be useful or rather useful. In addition, the staff expected the TNA system to improve patient care.[8] These and other results from the project confirm the assumption that the observed low staff turnover will persist. Since turnover is not solely dependent on individual motivation, but is also influenced by the environment, a general over- or underestimation of turnover is possible. This aspect, as well as regional conditions, should also be taken into account.

[8] See Kuntosch et al. (2020), p. 147.

**Table 5.1** Average costs per ambulance by year. *Source* Own representation. [As already shown in previous chapters, for the 4th and 5th year, 32 ambulances in regular operation and 10 ambulances as reserve vehicles (10 E) are included in the analysis.]

| | 1st year | 2nd year | 3rd year | 4th year | 5th year |
|---|---|---|---|---|---|
| total costs [€] | 1,468,483 | 1,486,770 | 1,505,606 | 2,063,601 | 1,961,280 |
| Number of advanced life support ambulances | 6 | 6 | 6 | 32+10 E | 32+10 E |
| **Average costs per advanced life support ambulance [€]** | **244,747** | **247,795** | **250,934** | **54,305** | **51,613** |

The proportion of costs for general system components relative to the annual total costs of the system has decreased in the scenario of an expansion to routine care. Here, too, the TNA system shows lower prices for all cost items from the fourth year onward (routine care). With the addition of new costs for uninterruptible power supply, the total costs in this category have increased. However, these largely uncontrollable fixed costs represent a smaller share in the event of a system expansion and no longer have as strong an impact on the total costs.

The following section presents the total costs for the first five years after system launch once again. Table 5.1 summarizes the results from the previous results chapters. First, the total costs per year and the number of advanced life support ambulances connected to the system in each scenario are shown. In the fourth year, the total costs increase by 37% for the routine care scenario and then decrease again. It should be noted that new investments are necessary to expand the TNA system (see Sect. 4.2.2.1). In addition, there are initial items for which depreciation has ended and for which no costs are incurred for the time being. If the system were implemented at the outset under the assumption of routine care, costs would already be higher in the first year and would then, as shown in the table, increase slightly each year.

Furthermore, the table presents the average costs per advanced life support ambulance (RTW). In the first three years of the project, during which only six ambulances were equipped with tele-emergency technology, the average total costs per ambulance amounted to approximately € 250,000 per year. The expansion of the system in the fourth year of observation (to a total of 42 ambulances) led to a significant reduction in average costs. The average costs per ambulance per year dropped to just over € 50,000. The expansion of the system thus brings substantial cost advantages, especially when it involves retrofitting and integrating additional TNA-equipped ambulances. This advantage will be illustrated by example below. First, the following two assumptions are made: (1) The incident statistics of the TNA suggest that an expansion to a total of 28 (+10) ambulances can be managed by a single operator. The staffing situation would therefore remain unchanged. (2) The tele-emergency doctor is part of standard care.

Using five alternatives for the number of ambulances included in the TNA system, it will be exemplified how total costs may develop depending on the number of ambulances and per ambulance.

| | |
|---|---|
| Variant "6" | Status quo: The number of ambulances equipped within the project framework remains at six. |
| Variant "6+2" | In addition to the six ambulances already equipped, two more ambulances are retrofitted. |
| Variant "6+11" | In addition to the six ambulances already equipped, a further eleven vehicles are equipped (corresponding to half of the remaining, not yet equipped ambulances in the district). |
| Variant "6+22" | In addition to the six ambulances already equipped, the remaining 22 ambulances (in regular operation) in V-G are equipped. |
| Variant "6+22+10E" | In addition to the six ambulances already equipped, the remaining 22 ambulances (in regular operation) as well as the 10 reserve vehicles of the district are equipped. |

Figure 5.1 shows the total costs for the five variants. Costs increase as the number of advanced life support ambulances in the system rises, with the average annual total costs per ambulance more than doubling from six to 38 ambulances in the system. Since the TNA system is analyzed as part of standard care, all system

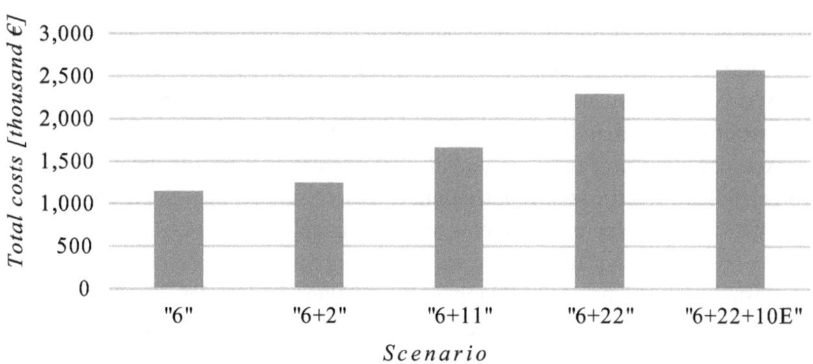


**Fig. 5.1** Total costs by scenario. *Source* Own illustration

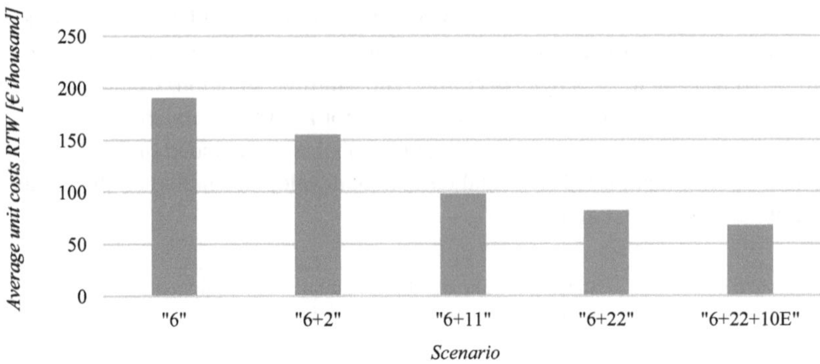


**Fig. 5.2** Average unit costs per ambulance. *Source* Own illustration

components relevant to this application were included. It is evident that total costs steadily increase with the number of equipped ambulances in the district. The increase in costs is due to the retrofitting of additional ambulances. The costs of all other system components remain constant, as in all alternatives a single TNA operates at one workstation.

When considering the average unit costs per retrofitted TNA ambulance, it becomes clear that costs decrease significantly from variant "6" to variant "6 + 22 + 10" (see Fig. 5.2). An advanced life support ambulance equipped with telemedicine equipment costs on average about € 190,000 per year when six ambulances are equipped. If a total of 38 ambulances are equipped (variant 6 + 22 + 10E), the unit costs drop to just under € 68,000 per tele-emergency-capable ambulance. These cost differences can be explained by the effect of fixed cost degression, as the proportion of fixed costs is high compared to variable costs when the TNA system transitions into standard care. The cost items classified as fixed costs are incurred in full in each of the five variants, regardless of the number of equipped ambulances. With a larger number of ambulances, the share of fixed costs per unit (i.e., per ambulance) decreases. The following cost items are considered fixed costs: uninterruptible power supply, tele-emergency doctor workstations, tele-emergency doctor training, annual material costs, proportional leasing costs for peeq®BOXes, as well as annual operating, personnel, and training costs independent of the number of ambulances. The results clearly show that equipping as many ambulances as possible brings a significant economic advantage. Nevertheless, annual total costs of approximately € 1.5–2 million are incurred, which must be financed.

To put the magnitude of these costs into a macroeconomic perspective, they can be compared with other alternatives in standard care. Another option, particularly for closing gaps in care in rural areas, would be to establish new emergency physician stations. The establishment of a new station can be estimated at around € 615,000 per year.[9] This figure for a single new station is well below the costs of introducing the TNA system. However, if it is assumed that a large area is to be covered by the TNA, it can be expected that several new NEF stations would need to be established. The costs for these would quickly exceed those of the telemedicine alternative. Additional problems would also arise, such as staffing these new stations with emergency physicians, since more personnel would be required for several stations than for staffing a single TNA center.

## 5.3 Transferability

The previous chapters have shown that the TNA system offers clear advantages for prehospital emergency rescue services. In particular, the cost benefits become evident with large-scale implementation of the system. However, this innovative care concept also incurs high annual costs. The establishment of a telemedicine system should therefore be carefully planned. Whether the system, as presented so far, can be transferred to other regions and which factors should be given special consideration will be discussed below.

In Sect. 4.2.3, a general standard cost function was established, providing an overview of the factors influencing the total costs of the system. In order to make a statement about the average total costs, the variables must be known or calculable. This allows the average total costs of a TNA system to be calculated based on the results from the Land|Rettung project. Nevertheless, the introduction of such a system should be well planned and many additional factors considered, since the standard cost function reflects the project situation in the district of V-G. The most important influencing factors will be discussed below.

In the district, 5.5 full-time equivalent positions were allocated for the 24/7 service of the tele-emergency physician. Depending on the call volume in a region, it may be possible not to provide the TNA service continuously in order to conserve resources. In Straubing (Bavaria), for example, the TNA service was only offered from approximately 7:30 a.m. to 7:30 p.m. For the district of V-G, the

[9] See Fleßa et al. (2016), p. 255.

results showed that the call volume was concentrated roughly between 8 a.m. and 11 p.m., with a peak between 9 a.m. and 12 p.m. Relatively few deployments occur during the night and early morning hours. Depending on whether this phenomenon is purely coincidental or has an underlying cause, it may be possible to suspend the use of the TNA during periods of generally low call volume. Based on the service hours in Straubing, however, it can be assumed that the low nighttime call volume observed in the district of V-G is not coincidental, but follows a similar pattern. If the TNA service is not to be offered 24 hours a day, this approach could offer potential for saving personnel costs, as the number of full-time equivalent positions could be adjusted. From an economic perspective, however, restricting the TNA service too much in terms of time could also have negative effects, since the majority of costs are incurred when the TNA system is introduced, regardless of how long the TNA office is staffed. In this context, savings would be limited solely to the salaries of additional staff. Given the ongoing shortage of personnel in some regions of Germany, a reduction in full-time equivalent positions would be advantageous, since the TNA position can only be filled by someone with the additional qualification "emergency medicine," a minimum of 500 emergency physician deployments, and a few other requirements.[10] The comparatively low call volume on a project basis, combined with the lack of direct patient or colleague contact, could make the position of tele-emergency physician less attractive, which may make recruitment more difficult. In such cases, appropriate incentives could be created to attract enough emergency physicians for the 24/7 TNA service. The number of TNAs to be deployed, as well as other emergency service staff, also determines the costs for the necessary training sessions.

When the system is introduced in a new region, the number of RTW to be retrofitted must first be determined. All ambulances in the region can be retrofitted, or, for example, only those at stations that are not in close proximity to an NEF station. In regions that are difficult for an NEF to reach, such as islands or very rural areas, the TNA could take on more deployments. When retrofitting a large number of ambulances, as in the district of V-G, price discounts appear to be possible. In addition, the previous chapter showed that it is advantageous to equip as many ambulances as possible with telemedicine technology when introducing the system, since the unit costs per ambulance decrease significantly due to the high proportion of system-related fixed costs (economies of scale). Furthermore, the 24/7 service offers the potential to support far more than the six ambulances

[10] See Kuntosch et al. (2020), p. 134 f.

involved in the project. Excessive restriction of the tele-emergency physician service to certain times of day or to a limited number of advanced life support ambulances would result in underutilization of the system and would not be efficient. The deployment situation is crucial here for the correct assessment and evaluation of the available operational readiness of a TNA. Depending on the number of ambulances in the system and the call volume, the number of necessary TNA workstations must be determined. The overload probability of the system calculated in Sect. 4.3 clearly demonstrated the capacity of a TNA workstation with only one tele-emergency physician on duty.

The introduction of the TNA system offers opportunities to counteract the increasing overload of prehospital emergency rescue services. The TNA is by no means intended to replace the conventional ground-based emergency physician, but rather to relieve and support them. The preceding chapters clearly show that the TNA is generally unable to manage severe cases, as the manual skills of an emergency physician at the patient's side are simply required. Nevertheless, the TNA is an important link between the care provided by the ambulance crew and the emergency physician. Here, the TNA can instruct, delegate, and advise when necessary. Its rapid operational readiness and constant availability are its unique features, which no ground-based emergency physician could provide. Thanks to the extensive capabilities, such as real-time transmission of the patient's vital data and visual communication options, the TNA can accurately assess deployment situations and thus offers a wide range of possible actions.

Connecting several regions to an already existing TNA system would additionally lead to significant synergy effects, especially with regard to costs. Most of the fixed costs are incurred per TNA system, regardless of how many ambulances are supported. Only when a threshold is reached, at which a second, parallel TNA is required to ensure that all deployments can be handled, would costs increase sharply. So far, different systems have been tested in different locations in Germany. Each region is testing its own stand-alone solution to address the developments in emergency rescue services. Only since 2020 has it become apparent that neighboring districts are willing to implement the existing TNA system. This is also the case in the district of Vorpommern-Rügen. Here, two ambulances were already equipped with telemedicine technology in February 2020. In the future, eleven advanced life support ambulances are to be connected to the TNA system in the district of V-G. This offers the major advantage that some of the system costs, such as the quality management system, the TNA workstation, and the annual licenses independent of the ambulances, do not incur additional expenses. Training can also be ensured, as already done for routine care in the district of V-G, through multipliers, since it is the same system.

Finally, this chapter will once again assess the costs in order to provide an overall economic evaluation of the TNA system. The annual costs of the TNA system currently amount to approximately 1.5 to 2 million euros. In the context of the project, these costs were covered by the Innovation Fund. Without secure financing, the system cannot be integrated into routine care. As part of the project, it was achieved that the health insurance funds committed to financing the introduction or transfer of the system into routine care in accordance with §12 RDG MV. When introducing the system in another district, it must be noted that the districts or independent cities must make advance payments, since the health insurance funds only reimburse the annual depreciation amount for material costs, meaning that the districts, at least in the federal state of Mecklenburg-Western Pomerania, must initially bear the costs themselves. The annual operating costs of the TNA system, such as license fees for ambulances and workstations, would, on the other hand, be continuously covered by the health insurance funds.[11] Legislation (RDG MV Chapter 2 §12 para. 2) further stipulates that usage fees are due for the deployment of emergency vehicles (such as ambulances and NEFs). These are renegotiated annually between service providers and payers. From 01.09.2020 to 31.12.2020, the fee for an ambulance was € 1020 and for an NEF € 995. The costs for the deployment are usually covered by the patient's health insurance. The results showed that the introduction of the TNA system led to an average of 4.5 fewer NEF deployments per day. As a comparative value, a brief calculation of the costs for the avoided deployments is provided. It is assumed that 4.5 deployments per day would result in a total of € 4477 in usage fees; over a year, this amounts to approximately 1.6 million euros for deployments that were mostly not life-threatening, as they could be handled by the tele-emergency physician. These costs roughly correspond to the annual costs of the TNA system. Of course, a more detailed analysis would require additional parameters, such as ambulance deployments and the examination of further relationships between the introduction of the TNA system and changes in the deployment structure. Nevertheless, this brief excursus already shows that conventional emergency rescue services incur high costs for health insurance funds and that the ongoing testing and evaluation of innovative care models is advantageous.

The results from the previous chapters show that the TNA system can certainly be transferred to other regions. In designing individual system components, regional factors such as call volume, personnel situation, and the network

[11] See Kuntosch et al. (2020), p. 235 ff.

of emergency stations must be taken into account. The variable components of the system influenced by these factors, such as the number of ambulances to be retrofitted or the TNA workstations, can be easily adjusted, which ultimately also changes the average total costs of the system. However, the fixed costs of the system remain largely constant, even when the system is expanded.

The system as presented in this work and established in the V-G district continues to offer many options for individual customization. For example, the TNA's service hours can be adjusted according to regional needs. It is also possible to systematically plan the selection of RTW to be included in the system, rather than converting an entire region at once. However, the advantages of equipping a large number of ambulances with telemedicine technology have been demonstrated. The effects of the system on the incident frequency of NEF and TNA, as well as the resulting deployment times, are difficult to predict, since other factors also influence these metrics, such as the motivation and acceptance of emergency medical service staff in general. If acceptance among paramedics, emergency medical technicians, or dispatch center staff is low, the TNA will be alerted less frequently and the effects will be diminished. Therefore, the introduction of the system should be accompanied from the outset by high motivation and involvement of emergency medical service staff in order to proactively address potential issues of low acceptance.

## 5.4 Opportunities and Risks of a Centralized TNA Service

As a potential system expansion, Sect. 4.3 examined the possibility of centralizing the telemedicine service.[12] The question arose as to whether there are advantages if several tele-emergency physicians work in parallel in a TNA office, thereby covering multiple regions and a large number of ambulances. Based on the mission data of the tele-emergency physician, the probability was calculated that a deployment cannot be accepted because the physician is already engaged and unable to take on additional cases. In this context, it was also examined how many TNAs would need to work in parallel to support a certain number of advanced life support ambulances. The results showed that the TNA in the V-G

[12] Based on the publication by Fleßa et al (2021) „Telemedical emergency services: central or decentral coordination?"

district, with six of the total 26 ambulances at the time of the study, still had available time capacity. Among other things, the probability of overload could be used for this purpose, which, under the conditions during the project period, was very low at 0.03%. The results indicated that even a significant expansion of the system to include many more telemedicine-equipped ambulances would only slightly increase this probability. The TNA system thus demonstrates clear potential for application and expansion, as the TNA is only very rarely fully occupied with two simultaneous deployments and therefore unable to accept another. Compared to the ground-based emergency physician, who can only attend to one case at a time, personnel resources in the TNA system can be used more efficiently.

With regard to the results presented, it should also be considered that the data basis for the queuing model was limited to the period with the highest number of telemedicine deployments for the arrival rate, so that the actual workload is to be regarded as above average compared to other times of day. Deployments with a mission duration between one minute and under three hours were included. The actual arrival rate of deployments throughout the day is 0.17 per hour, which is significantly lower than the 0.27 per hour assumed in the model for the period between 9 a.m. and 12 p.m. The model thus represents a scenario of maximum workload. In reality, the workload of the TNA and thus the probability of system overload due to simultaneous deployments will be lower, since a constant arrival rate corresponding to the observed peak cannot be assumed throughout the day. Depending on the time of day selected for analysis, the system parameters of the queue (arrival and service rates) will change slightly. For optimal use of the system, it would even be desirable to support as many advanced life support ambulances as possible, so that capacity is fully utilized and available resources are used efficiently.

The positive effects of the TNA system on the deployment structure in prehospital emergency care in the V-G district and the cost advantages over other supplementary care concepts have already been discussed in detail in previous chapters and remain relevant for the question of centralization or decentralization of the system. When considering the organization of the complex telemedicine system, additional aspects arise, which will be discussed for both alternatives below.

The results showed that the costs of a centralized TNA system are lower than those of a decentralized solution. In particular, the costs for the entire system and for each region are significantly lower with centralization than with a decentralized approach. This becomes especially clear when looking in detail at the individual cost items.

Setting up a TNA workstation involves costs of approximately € 24,000. In addition, annual license fees of around € 72,000 per workstation are incurred, which are also independent of the chosen alternative. However, the main cost driver for the workstation is not the material or operating costs, but personnel costs. For 24-hour service, 365 days a year, at least five tele-emergency physicians are required, resulting in total annual costs of € 631,004. If several TNA offices are operated simultaneously (one per region – decentralized), the aforementioned personnel costs are incurred for each. In contrast, if only one central office with one or a few physicians is operated, personnel costs are lower. A 24/7 central office with 5.5 FTEs can cover the same number of deployments as several regions, each of which would require 5.5 FTEs for TNA in a decentralized setup. From an economic perspective, establishing fewer workstations with a smaller total staff is more advantageous than setting up TNA workstations across the board.

The challenges already described several times regarding the staffing of physician positions underscore this issue and argue in favor of centralization. Physicians are a scarce resource in Germany, and emergency physicians with specialized training in emergency medicine and telemedicine are particularly rare. Many highly qualified physicians also prefer to work in cities rather than rural areas.[13] Regardless of the costs involved, it is possible that the number of tele-emergency physicians required for a decentralized solution is simply not available on the market. Tele-emergency physicians could, if they wished, live and work in cities while still providing care for emergencies in rural areas. Centralization would also make the management of the TNA office and the entire emergency medical system simpler and more efficient.

Since the system's workload in this study is considered low, the system is capable of much more if additional ambulances are integrated. Especially with regard to staffing multiple telemedicine offices at low utilization, this could be considered a waste of resources. In the decentralized solution, many highly qualified tele-emergency physicians would spend a large portion of their shifts "waiting" for a deployment. While all emergency service personnel are affected by such "waiting" and are characterized by high personnel commitment, the TNA's deployment rate, at 4.5 per day, is significantly lower than the approximately 66 deployments per day for ambulances and NEF (in the model region). The shorter mission duration for the TNA also leads to lower utilization and thus to longer daily "waiting times" for a deployment. In a centralized solution,

[13] See Kaduszkiewicz et al. (2018), p. 187 ff.

where tele-emergency physicians supervise a larger number of TNA-equipped ambulances and thus accompany more deployments, a learning process can be expected for both medical and non-medical staff. The anticipated economies of scale will have a positive effect on the quality of care provided by the TNA and, in the long term, lead to an improvement in the quality of care delivered by tele-emergency physicians. Ultimately, the entire prehospital emergency care system will benefit from this learning process associated with the new model of care.

A large, centralized TNA office with multiple TNAs offers an additional advantage in terms of better coordination, for example, in the event of acute illness of a tele-emergency physician on duty. When many tele-emergency physicians work together in an office with several parallel workstations, the likelihood of finding staff for vacation coverage, night and weekend shifts, as well as during holiday periods, increases. The 24/7 service would be better secured, as more colleagues would be available to take over or fill in for shifts. In addition, the quality of telemedicine deployments is likely to improve after centralization. If more than one TNA works in an office, they can support each other in the event of an emergency or a particularly difficult case. The introduction of specialization among TNAs is also conceivable in a centralized TNA office, for example in the field of pediatrics. In this way, deployment support could be optimized in the long term.

Another advantage of the centralized solution is found in the pricing of individual system components. Procuring large quantities can lead to volume discounts from service providers and have a positive effect on the total costs of the centralized TNA office. It is also conceivable that training sessions would be less expensive with a larger number of trainees in one office than if smaller groups were trained separately. In the decentralized solution, joint training across regions would result in high travel costs and might no longer be economically viable.

There are many aspects that speak in favor of centralizing the system. Nevertheless, there are also advantages to a decentralized TNA system, which will also be discussed below.

The introduction or expansion of the system to include many regional TNA offices offers the advantage that the tele-emergency physicians possess local knowledge. This allows information about locations, road infrastructure, and familiarity with medical facilities to be incorporated into the emergency rescue services and communication with the ambulance crew. The TNA can delegate tasks to the paramedics on site more easily, as they are more familiar with local conditions than a tele-emergency physician who is working from an office hundreds of kilometers away and is unfamiliar with the area. Therefore, in a decentralized solution, tele-emergency physicians can make decisions based on insights that take into account comprehensive knowledge of the local situation. While it could be argued that the ambulance crew can convey this knowledge to the TNA during an operation, this would take more time and carries the risk of information loss. Thus, a decentralized system could lead to better outcomes.

An advantage of the centralized system that has been discussed is the increased utilization of tele-emergency physicians. For optimal resource use, it is necessary for the TNA system to be well utilized, which leads to a higher workload for the tele-emergency physicians. As the number of ambulances integrated into the system increases, the number of deployments rises, reducing the "waiting time" between calls and ultimately increasing the likelihood of overload. The consequences of sustained high workloads can manifest as stress, high turnover, and, conversely, increasing difficulties in recruiting personnel. In comparison, too low a workload for tele-emergency physicians in decentralized offices could lead to boredom and also make the TNA position appear unattractive. To what extent these two perspectives on workload will affect the TNA service is currently unclear and would need to be examined over the long term in different scenarios.

The implementation hurdles in introducing telemedicine systems, such as the need for a robust network infrastructure, were outlined at the beginning of this work (Sect. 2.4.3). In the event of a widespread system failure, the decentralized organization of the TNA service has the advantage that telemedical emergency care does not fail across the board. The risk of such an existential scenario—such as fire, prolonged power outages, or strikes—is low but still present. This risk could be mitigated by providing reserve capacities, which, however, would lead to higher costs for the centralized solution.

The management of a decentralized system could also be more efficient, as the tele-emergency physicians and ambulance crews know each other and can build mutual trust. This can accelerate the service process,[14] as, for example, communication between the parties involved can also be optimized. The TNA could even tailor decisions to the known abilities of individual paramedics. Flexibility may also increase if the tele-emergency physicians are familiar with local conditions, as their familiarity with current circumstances (e.g., detours, weather, events) enables them to respond to the local situation.

Germany is a federal republic, and emergency systems are entirely under the authority of the state governments. This means that there are 16 different emergency service laws in Germany, each with varying regulations regarding the

[14] See Fleßa et al. (2021), p. 10.

rights and duties of paramedics, specific features of the rescue chain (e.g., use of helicopters), and limits on deployment times. For tele-emergency physicians in a highly centralized office, it is difficult to know all the regulations of the different federal states, keep track of them, and ultimately supervise the various staff members during operations according to the correct legal requirements. Undoubtedly, some of the disadvantages of the centralized system can be addressed through professional software support, such as detailed online information about weather conditions and legal regulations. However, keeping this information up to date is likely to require significant effort (in terms of personnel and time), which in turn leads to additional costs that have not been included in previous cost calculations.

Not only should the advantages and disadvantages for the tele-emergency physicians be discussed, but also possible effects on patients. Results from the Land|Rettung project showed generally high acceptance and satisfaction with the TNA system. When considering the question of a centralized system, in which the tele-emergency physician is not located in the region of the incident, acceptance could suffer, especially in rural areas. Here, it is particularly older people in villages who may not have strong technical skills and therefore cannot identify with new technologies. The resulting discomfort, combined with the desire for personal contact with a physician, can negatively affect patient acceptance. For older patients in particular, it will make a difference whether the ambulance crew explains that the TNA is located in the same district or hundreds of kilometers away in a major city.

A number of advantages and disadvantages for the alternatives of a central versus a decentralized organization of the TNA office could be identified. Table 5.2 provides an overview of the individual aspects and contrasts the respective pros and cons.

The various advantages and disadvantages of both alternatives clearly show that neither is superior in all respects. Therefore, an intermediate solution would be ideal, in which several regions are each served centrally by a TNA office. In this way, the advantages of both variants could be combined to leverage the economic benefits of the central solution. One conceivable approach would be to establish an additional two to three tele-emergency physician offices in Germany in regions with high population density and ambulance demand, alongside the TNA office in Greifswald,[15] in order to maintain the character of centralization. Another option would be to have more TNA offices distributed across Germany

[15] See Fleßa et al. (2021), p. 11.

**Table 5.2** Advantages and disadvantages of centralization. *Source* Fleßa (2021)

| *Criteria* | *Subcriteria* | *Advantage* | *Disadvantage* |
|---|---|---|---|
| Costs | Equipment and facilities | Higher utilization leads to lower costs per service unit | |
| | Personnel | Higher utilization leads to lower costs per service unit | |
| | Economies of scale | Learning effects lead to lower costs per service unit | |
| Quality | Local knowledge | | No detailed knowledge of location, infrastructure, and specific local features |
| | Safety | TNAs can support each other in complex situations | |
| | Learning effects | Greater routine, subspecialization of TNAs | |
| | Existential risks | | Collapse of the central system means collapse for all districts |
| Administration | Team cohesion | | A decentralized system leads to greater trust between ambulance crews and TNAs, as well as better knowledge of each partner's strengths and weaknesses |
| | Personnel | Fewer TNAs required | Stress for TNAs |
| | Further training | Economies of scale | |
| | Flexibility | Flexible staffing (e.g., at night, on weekends, during holidays, in cases of unexpected illness) | Inflexible response to changes in local parameters |
| Structures | Laws and regulations | | Different emergency service laws in the federal states |
| Patients | Patient trust | | Greater trust when the distance to the TNA is smaller |

as smaller central units. For example, each federal state could be served by a TNA center. It is essential that the capacity of a TNA office is fully utilized to enable efficient and resource-saving operations.

Even the small federal state of Mecklenburg-Western Pomerania, with eight districts, 1.6 million inhabitants, and a population density of 69 people per square kilometer, would benefit significantly from a central system. Instead of costs amounting to approximately € 696,900 per district, centralizing eight districts in one office would result in costs per district of about € 87,100 (assuming that 23% of all ambulances are equipped with telemedicine technology) or about € 224,100 (assuming that all ambulances are equipped with telemedicine technology).

## 5.5 Limitations

The present study, along with its underlying datasets and methodology, is multi-faceted. Therefore, at the conclusion of this work, the applied methodology will be critically examined once more, and potential limitations will be identified and discussed.

In particular, the analysis of the deployment statistics is based on a very large data set from the emergency medical services software. The multi-stage plausibility check described in Sect. 3.3.2.1 was developed step by step based on data review and, due to the volume of records, had to be conducted separately for individual years or even quarters. The cleaned datasets were only merged again afterwards. Each step of the plausibility check was documented in detail for all quarters and years to ensure consistent validation of all records over the entire period. While technical solutions (e.g., the creation of an automated program script) could have supported the validation process, it was instead carried out using individual formulas in Excel. This approach does not rule out errors during data validation, as manual solutions are generally more error-prone than technical ones. However, it can be assumed that the deletion of plausible or the retention of implausible records in small numbers does not affect the overall results, since the data set, with nearly 250,000 records, can be considered very large and representative. The results also showed that, given the wide dispersion of data values, the median is the more appropriate measure for interpreting the results.

The data on secondary deployments already showed a significant increase from one year to the next, which could not be explained within the scope of this study (see Sect. 4.1.1). One possible reason for this uncertainty could be that the data over the observation period was provided by different individuals, and, for example, filter settings may have inadvertently differed. The data should have been checked for such inconsistencies immediately after export, before they were no longer accessible in the system. However, since the sharp increase in secondary mission data only became apparent from the fourth quarter of 2017, the relevant datasets were already two years old.

The presented planned costs and calculations also always refer to the data from the model region and should be regarded as exemplary for this specific case. Some aspects that can influence the level of costs have already been presented and discussed in Sect. 5.2 (e.g., regional characteristics, providers, purchase volumes, or service models). The results presented can therefore only serve as a guideline for costs and cost allocation and cannot be directly transferred to other regions without further adjustments. The personnel situation, for example, is specific to the model region, as staff are provided by the University Medical Center Greifswald. In a different setup, such as a centralized TNA office, tele-emergency physicians would be specifically hired to staff the office, and they might not have such diverse qualifications, which would affect personnel costs, as would regionally varying collective agreements for staff.

The costs in the model, especially fixed costs such as rent, quality management, and supervision, are based on the assumption that they do not depend on the number of tele-emergency physicians working in parallel. However, if a large number of tele-emergency physicians were to work simultaneously in one office (centralization), it can be assumed that costs would change, as, for example, larger premises would need to be rented. It may also be necessary to employ several supervisors to oversee the tele-emergency medical service. In the case of partial centralization, where several TNA offices are established nationwide, the critical number of ambulances and thus required TNA could be reached, at which point fixed costs would increase sharply. This threshold has not yet been reached in the analyses. Therefore, the defined fixed costs in the comparison of both alternatives should not be considered definitively fixed, as this could lead to an overestimation of the cost advantages of centralization.

To analyze the capacity utilization of the TNA system, a queuing model was used to examine the potential for centralization. The model is based on various assumptions that must be critically reviewed. While Fleßa et al. (2021) demonstrated that arrivals are Markov-distributed, the distribution for service times was only assumed in this analysis. A different distribution (e.g., based on a new data set) could lead to changes in the results. However, only numerical changes, not fundamental changes in the results or their interpretation, are to be expected.

Furthermore, the model parameters are based on peak times with the highest arrival rates. In reality, the arrival rate is consistently lower throughout the day than the one used. Depending on which times of day are used to determine the arrival rate of deployments, the arrival rate will adjust accordingly. The chosen methodology may underestimate the advantages of centralization at other times of day, meaning that centralization could be more cost-effective during periods when TNA utilization is even lower.

Various limitations are evident in the present study. Some issues could be more sharply focused through further analyses and avoided by adjusting the methodological approach.

# 6 Conclusion and Outlook

This paper presents the evaluation results of the introduction of an innovative care concept involving a telemedicine system in prehospital emergency care. The focus was on analyzing changes in incident statistics, determining the costs of the system, as well as examining the questions of transferability and optimization.

The potential of the TNA system as a valuable complement to conventional preclinical emergency care became evident, aligning with the original objectives of the Land|Rettung project. The implementation of the system in rural areas has not previously been realized to this extent and represents a significant milestone. The expansion and integration of the TNA system into the standard care of the V-G district further supports this finding. Since rural areas are particularly affected by staff shortages, low population density, and long response distances, the telemedicine system can help overcome barriers to patient care. In cases where the NEF has a very long response time and the RTW can arrive comparatively quickly, the patient can be treated faster by the TNA than by the NEF. The TNA can bridge the therapy-free interval until the emergency doctor arrives on site, or, as the data show, this interval can be shortened and treatment can be provided entirely without an emergency doctor. Paramedics can administer medication to patients with legal certainty via the TNA connection, even in the absence of a conventional emergency doctor.[1] The TNA system had little impact on the response time limit. Individual cases would need to be considered and analyzed here. However, it is also important to critically note the stationing of telemedicine-equipped RTWs. A different distribution to even more rural areas of the district might have produced different effects.

[1] See Kuntosch et al. (2020), p. 163 f.



R. Süss, *The Tele-Emergency Physician System as an Innovation in Prehospital Emergency Care*, https://doi.org/10.1007/978-3-658-49561-9_6

Emergency medical services are characterized by “waiting” for an emergency. An excessive reduction in the daily number of deployments, for example by distributing cases across many emergency physician stations, could lead to underutilization of personnel. In addition, such expansion results in unnecessarily high costs. The emergency doctor resource would not be used efficiently. The TNA offers great potential here, as its comparatively short engagement and rapid, constant availability make it more efficient from a time perspective, especially in non-life-threatening cases. The risk that a patient has to wait unnecessarily long for treatment because no emergency physician is available due to being engaged elsewhere is also reduced. Overall, the introduction of the TNA system led to a reduction in NEF deployments, which in turn resulted in cost savings for health insurers and thus economic benefits overall.

The analyses also showed from an economic perspective that the TNA system is dominant compared to other alternatives. The costs of establishing new emergency physician stations, for example, would exceed the annual costs of the TNA system if implemented on a large scale in emergency care. The telemedicine advantages of consultation, second opinions, and digital networking to guidelines, for example, would not be realized. Especially with regard to staffing in rural regions, it should be easier, despite the extensive training required for tele-emergency physicians, to fill a few positions rather than to find enough personnel to staff numerous stations across a wide area. The TNA system’s ability to decouple the “workplace” from the place of residence and offer flexible work arrangements is particularly positive for many employees.

To date, there are hardly any publications in the literature on cost analyses in preclinical emergency rescue services with comparable scope and level of detail. However, analyses in this area should not be underestimated from a macroeconomic perspective. The costs of emergency services already amounted to 6,539 million euros in 2020 and are increasing annually. Ongoing attention to these costs is highly relevant and necessary to identify new optimization potentials. The testing of new forms of care can make a decisive contribution in this regard.

Digitalization is steadily advancing. Many people use the internet, enabling them to access a wide range of digital services in all areas of life and benefit from their advantages. Emergency rescue services can and should also take advantage of these benefits. The Land|Rettung project serves as an example and clearly demonstrates that the majority of patients showed high acceptance of the new form of care after only a short period of system operation. The medical evaluation results from the project also clearly show that staff quickly became familiar with the use of the TNA system. In the model region, employees rotate between stations and reported that in certain situations they would like to have audio and visual communication with the TNA when working in an RTW not equipped for TNA.[2] The high medical quality of the TNA system was also confirmed through surveys. The TNA system itself is therefore a targeted extension and enhancement of preclinical emergency care and brings many advantages.

When deciding to introduce the system, it is essential to consider that additional, especially economic, benefits (fixed cost degression) can be realized by deploying the system across the board. The cost differences between the centralized and decentralized alternatives were extensively presented and discussed in this paper. Comprehensive implementation of the system is more cost-effective (unit costs per region) with a centralized service. However, the specific design of the system depends on various regional factors (incident statistics, population, staffing, legal framework, etc.). A combination of both alternatives could generate synergy effects (personnel costs, capacity utilization, fixed costs, network infrastructure, system interfaces, etc.) if the same system is introduced even with decentralized coordination. Later consolidation of several areas would then encounter fewer obstacles. A realistic assessment and agreement on an acceptable maximum overload probability (e.g., 5%, 10%, or 20%) for the tele-emergency physician service appears to be a challenge that would also need to be addressed from a political perspective. In the long term, empirical data from regions with telemedicine applications could serve as a basis for this.

The application of operations research methods, as presented in this paper, clearly demonstrates that complex issues can be analyzed from a business management perspective. Based on empirical data from emergency medical services, it was possible to derive results using a queuing model that support decision-makers in emergency medical services demand planning. Furthermore, the results can be used to generate recommendations for action that can lead to optimal allocation of scarce resources. The application of business management principles and methods to a complex, practice-oriented topic such as preclinical emergency care by emergency medical services is effective for process optimization while taking cost structures into account.

The TNA system, as introduced in the V-G district, is already showing positive effects on emergency rescue services. The identified weaknesses, particularly regarding the expansion of the system, were also presented and can be taken into account when implementing it in other districts or federal states. Which strategy individual regions will pursue remains to be seen. The tele-emergency physician,

[2] See Kuntosch et al. (2020), p. 165.

as part of digitalization, offers a good opportunity to counteract the increasing challenges in emergency care and to ease the worsening situation. Acceptance among patients, emergency service providers, and health insurers was demonstrated within the project. The advantages of a comprehensive rollout of the system, as opposed to continuing to test isolated solutions, are clear.

# References

**§193ff AO, §7 Abs 1 EStG**, AfA-Tabelle für die allgemein verwendbaren Anlagegüter. Online verfügbar unter https://www.bundesfinanzministerium.de/Web/DE/Themen/Steuern/Steuerverwaltungu-Steuerrecht/Betriebspruefung/AfA_Tabellen/afa_tabellen.html, zuletzt geprüft am 05.06.2022.

**Ahnefeld, F.** (1990), Notfallmedizin, 2. korrigierte Auflage, Berlin.

**Atzbach, U.; Hündorf, H.-P.; Lipp, R. (eds.)** (2016), Notfallsanitäter upgrade. Vorbereitung auf die Ergänzungsprüfung, 2. aktualisierte und ergänzte Auflage, Stumpf + Kossendey Verlagsgesellschaft mbH.

**Braga, A. V.** (2018), Die telemedizinische Konsultation. In: M. A. Pfannstiel, A. Focke und H. Mehlich (eds.): Management von Gesundheitsregionen IV, pp. 92–108, Wiesbaden.

**Brinkrolf, P.; Laslo, T.; Fischer, L.; Hasebrook, J.; Hahnenkamp, K.; Günther, J. et al.** (2020), Das Projekt Land|Rettung und sein Hintergrund. In: K. Hahnenkamp, S. Fleßa, J. Hasebrook, P. Brinkrolf, B. Metelmann und C. Metelmann (eds.): Notfallversorgung auf dem Land. Ergebnisse des Pilotprojektes Land|Rettung, 1st edn, pp. 1–22, Berlin.

**Brinkrolf, P.; Scheer, D.; Hasebrook, J.; Hahnenkamp, K.** (2017), Land|Rettung – zukunftsfähige notfallmedizinische Neuausrichtung eines Landkreises. In: V. E. Amelung, S. Eble, H. Hildebrandt, F. Knieps, R. Lägel, S. Ozegowski et al. (eds.): Innovationsfonds. Impulse für das deutsche Gesundheitssystem, pp. 140–145, Berlin.

**Brokmann, J.; Felzen, M; Beckers, S.; Czaplik, M.; Hirsch, F.; Bergrath, S.; Rossaint, R.** (2017), Telemedizin: Potenziale in der Notfallmedizin. In: *Notf.med. up2date* 12 (03), pp. 307–317. https://doi.org/10.1055/s-0043-116700.

**Brokmann, J. C.; Rossaint, R.; Bergrath, S.; Valentin, B.; Beckers, S. K.; Hirsch, F. et al.** (2015), Potenzial und Wirksamkeit eines telemedizinischen Rettungsassistenzsystems: Prospektive observationelle Studie zum Einsatz in der Notfallmedizin. Prospektive observationelle Studie zum Einsatz in der Notfallmedizin. In: *Der Anaesthesist* 64 (6), pp. 438–445. https://doi.org/10.1007/s00101-015-0039-1.

**Bundesärztekammer** (2013), Indikationskatalog für den Notarzteinsatz. Online verfügbar unter https://www.bundesaerztekammer.de/aerzte/versorgung/notfallmedizin/notarzt/indikationskatalog-fuer-den-notarzteinsatz/, zuletzt geprüft am 25.07.2022.



R. Süss, *The Tele-Emergency Physician System as an Innovation in Prehospital Emergency Care,* https://doi.org/10.1007/978-3-658-49561-9

**Bundesärztekammer** (2015), Telemedizinische Methoden in der Patientenversorgung – Begriffliche Verortung. Online verfügbar unter https://www.bundesaerztekammer.de/aerzte/telematiktelemedizin/telemedizin/, zuletzt geprüft am 25.07.2022.

**Bundesinstitut für Bevölkerungsforschung** (2021), Bevölkerungsdichte in Deutschland nach Kreisen 2019. Unter Mitarbeit von Statistisches Bundesamt. Online verfügbar unter https://www.bib.bund.de/DE/Fakten/Fakt/B77-Bevoelkerungsdichte-Kreise.html, zuletzt geprüft am 10.09.2021.

**Czaplik, M.; Bergrath, S.** (2016), Telemedizin in der Notfallmedizin. In: F. Fischer und A. Krämer (eds.): eHealth in Deutschland. Anforderungen und Potenziale innovativer Versorgungsstrukturen, pp. 319–333, Berlin.

**Deutscher Bundestag** (2016), Organisation der Notfallversorgung in Deutschland unter besonderer Berücksichtigung des Rettungsdienstes und des Ärztlichen Bereitschaftsdienstes (105/15). Online verfügbar unter https://www.google.com/url?sa=t&rct=j&q=&esrc=s&source=web&cd=&ved=2ahUKEwik8aykgLz4AhWrS_EDHf-LDEAQFnoECAkQAQ&url=https%3A%2F%2Fwww.bundestag.de%2Fresource%2b%2F408406%2F0e3ec79bfb78d7dde0c659a2be0927ca%2Fwd-9%25E2%25803105%25E2%2580%259314%25E2%2580%2593pdf-data.pdf&usg=AOvVaw0uUrwV2_M3rsNFxE7w2y9j, zuletzt geprüft am 20.06.2022.

**Eichhorn, P.; Merk, J.** (2016), Das Prinzip Wirtschaftlichkeit. Basiswissen der Betriebswirtschaftslehre, 4. vollständig überarb. Auflage, Wiesbaden.

**Eiff, W. von; Dodt, C.; Brachmann, M.; Niehues, C.; Fleischmann, T. (eds.)** (2016), Management der Notaufnahme. Patientenorientierung und optimale Ressourcennutzung als strategischer Erfolgsfaktor, Stuttgart.

**Fleßa, S.** (2014), Die Zukunft der Krankenhäuser im ländlichen Raum – findet statt! In: F. Dünkel, M. Herbst und T. Schlegel (eds.): Think Rural!, pp. 53–63, Wiesbaden.

**Fleßa, S.; Krohn, M.; Scheer, D.; Hahnenkamp, K.** (2016), Der Telenotarzt als Innovation des Rettungswesens im ländlichen Raum – eine gesundheitsökonomische Analyse für den Kreis Vorpommern-Greifswald. In: *Die Unternehmung* 70 (3), pp. 248–262. https://doi.org/10.5771/0042-059X-2016-3-248.

**Fleßa, S.; Süss, R.; Kuntosch, J.; Krohn, M.; Metelmann, B.; Hasebrook, J.-P. et al.** (2021), Telemedical emergency services: central or decentral coordination? In: *Health economics review* 11 (1), p. 7. https://doi.org/10.1186/s13561-021-00303-5.

**Gorgaß, B.** (2003), Die Klinik als zentrales Glied der Rettungskette. In: *Notfall Rettungsmed* 6 (8), pp. 559–563. https://doi.org/10.1007/s10049-003-0615-9.

**Grünstäudl, M.** (2013), Praxishandbuch Kostenrechnung. Grundlagen, Prozesse, Systeme, Konstanz.

**Hahnenkamp, K.; Fleßa, S.; Hasebrook, J.; Brinkrolf, P.; Metelmann, B.; Metelmann, C. (eds.)** (2020), Notfallversorgung auf dem Land. Ergebnisse des Pilotprojektes Land|Rettung, 1st edn, Berlin.

**Hedtstück, U.** (2013), Simulation diskreter Prozesse. Methoden und Anwendungen, Berlin.

**Hellmich, C. (ed.)** (2010), Qualitätsmanagement und Zertifizierung im Rettungsdienst. Grundlagen – Techniken – Modelle – Umsetzung, Berlin.

**Humburg, D.; Timpe, M.; Wranze-Bielefeld, E.; Martens, F.; Rupp, D.; Sassen, M. C.** (2021), Der Telenotarzt als „Einsatzleiter" zur Stabilisierung eines kritisch kranken

Patienten. In: *Notfall & Rettungsmedizin*, pp. 1–6. https://doi.org/10.1007/s10049-021-00945-2.

**Justizministerium Mecklenburg-Vorpommern** (01.05.2015), Rettungsdienstgesetz Mecklenburg-Vorpommern. RDG MV, vom 09.02.2015. Fundstelle: GVOBI. M-V 2015, 50.

**Justizministerium Mecklenburg-Vorpommern** (08.10.2016), Verordnung über die Rettungsdienstplanung und weitere Ausführung des Rettungsdienstgesetztes Mecklenburg-Vorpommern. RDPVO MV, vom 26.09.2016. Fundstelle: GVOBI.M-V 2016, 799, pp. 799–809.

**Kaduszkiewicz, H.; Teichert, U.; van den Bussche, H.** (2018), Ärztemangel in der hausärztlichen Versorgung auf dem Lande und im Öffentlichen Gesundheitsdienst: Eine kritische Analyse der Evidenz bezüglich der Rolle von Aus- und Weiterbildung. In: *Bundesgesundheitsblatt, Gesundheitsforschung, Gesundheitsschutz* 61 (2), pp. 187–194, https://doi.org/10.1007/s00103-017-2671-1.

**Koncz, V.; Kohlmann, T.; Bielmeier, S.; Urban, B.; Prückner, S.** (2019), Telenotarzt : Neues Versorgungskonzept in der Notfallmedizin. In: *Unfallchirurg* 122 (9), pp. 683–689. https://doi.org/10.1007/s00113-019-0679-8.

**Kraft, M.** (2018), Telemedizin. In: Karl-Heinrich Grote, Beate Bender und Dietmar Göhlich (eds.): Dubbel, p. 702, Berlin.

**Kühn, D.; Aechter, J.; Weidringer, W.** (eds.) (2010), Rettungsdienst heute, 5th edn, München.

**Kuntosch, J.; Brinkrolf, P.; Metelmann, C.; Metelmann, B.; Fischer, L.; Hirsch, F. et al.** (2020), Etablierung einer Telenotarzt-Anwendung. In: K. Hahnenkamp, S. Fleßa, J. Hasebrook, P. Brinkrolf, B. Metelmann und C. Metelmann (eds.): Notfallversorgung auf dem Land. Ergebnisse des Pilotprojektes Land|Rettung, 1st edn, pp. 115–246, Berlin.

**Lohs, T.; Wnent, J.; Jakisch, B.** (2018), Dokumentation und Qualitätsmanagement im Rettungsdienst. In: *Notf.med. up2date* 13 (04), pp. 391–406. https://doi.org/10.1055/a-0587-8830.

**Marx, G.; Rossaint, R.; Marx, N.** (2021), Telemedizin, Berlin.

**Meyer, M.; Hansen, K.** (1996), Planungsverfahren des Operations Research. Für Wirtschaftswissenschaftler, Informatiker und Ingenieure, 4. vollständig überarbeitete Auflage, München.

**Niehues, C.** (2012), Notfallversorgung in Deutschland. Analyse des Status quo und Empfehlungen für ein patientenorientiertes und effizientes Notfallmanagement. Zugl.: Münster (Westfalen), Univ., Diss., 2011. 1st edn, Stuttgart.

**Nolting, H.-D.; Zich, K.** (2017), Telemedizinische Prozessinnovationen in den Regelbetrieb. Lessons Learned. Online verfügbar unter https://www.bertelsmann-stiftung.de/de/publikationen/publikation/did/telemedizinische-prozessinnovationen-in-den-regelbetrieb, zuletzt geprüft am 25.07.2022.

**o.V.** (1999), Technische Richtlinie der Behörden und Organisationen mit Sicherheitsaufgaben (BOS). Funkmeldesystem, pp. 1–73, Münster.

**o.V.** (2017), Minimaler Notfalldatensatz MIND3.1. Codierte Werte. Online verfügbar unter https://www.divi.de/empfehlungen/qualitaetssicherung-intensivmedizin/mind-notfall-einsatzprotokoll, zuletzt geprüft am 27.07.2022.

**Pfannstiel, M. A.; Da-Cruz, P.; Mehlich, H.** (2017), Digitale Transformation von Dienstleistungen im Gesundheitswesen I, Wiesbaden.

**Plötner, O.; Sieben, B.; Kummer, T.-F.** (2010), Kosten- und Erlösrechnung. Anschaulich, kompakt, praxisnah, 2. korrigierte und aktualisierte Auflage, Berlin.

**Prasser, C.; Süss, R.; Hahnenkamp, K.; Hasebrook, J.; Brinkrolf, P.; Fleßa, S.** (2020), Der Telenotarzt als Innovation des Rettungsdienstes im ländlichen Raum – Kosten der Implementierung. In: *Gesundheitsökonomie & Qualitätsmanagement* 25 (03), pp. 150–156. https://doi.org/10.1055/a-1080-6792.

**Rajan, S.; Wissenberg, M.; Folke, F.; Hansen, S. M.; Gerds, T. A.; Kragholm, K. et al.** (2016), Association of Bystander Cardiopulmonary Resuscitation and Survival According to Ambulance Response Times After Out-of-Hospital Cardiac Arrest. In: *Circulation* 134 (25), pp. 2095–2104. https://doi.org/10.1161/CIRCULATIONAHA.116.024400.

**Reimann, B.; Maier, B. C.; Lott, R.; Konrad, F.** (2004), Gefährdung der Notarztversorgung im ländlichen Gebiet. Bericht über das 3. Sigmaringer Symposium für Notfallmedizin am 22.11.2003. In: *Notfall Rettungsmed* 7 (3). https://doi.org/10.1007/s10049-004-0656-8.

**Ried, W.** (2016), Gesundheitsversorgung im ländlichen Raum: Ziele und Indikatoren. In: M. Herbst, F. Dünkel und B. Stahl (eds.): Daseinsvorsorge und Gemeinwesen im ländlichen Raum, pp. 1–23, Wiesbaden.

**Rossaint, R.; Wolff, J.; Lapp, N.; Hirsch, F.; Bergrath, S.; Beckers, S. K. et al.** (2017), Indikationen und Grenzen des Telenotarztsystems. In: *Notfall Rettungsmed* 20 (5), pp. 410–417. https://doi.org/10.1007/s10049-016-0259-1.

**Schlechtriemen, T.; Dirks, B.; Lackner, C.-K.; Moecke, H.; Blumenberg, D.** (2007), Wirtschaftlichkeit im Rettungsdienst. In: *Notfall Rettungsmed* 10 (8), pp. 589–592. https://doi.org/10.1007/s10049-007-0984-6.

**Schlömer, C.; Spangenberg, M.** (2009), Stätisch und ländlich geprägte Räume: Gemeinsamkeiten und Gegensätze, Bonn.

**Schmiedel, R.; Behrendt, H.** (2019), Leistungen des Rettungsdienstes. Analyse des Leistungsniveaus im Rettungsdienst für die Jahre 2016 und 2017, Heft M 290, Bremen.

**Schmiedel, R.; Behrendt, H.; Betzler, E.** (2012), Regelwerk zur Bedarfsplanung Rettungsdienst, Witten.

**Schneider, T.; Wolcke, B.; Böhmer, R. (eds.)** (2006), Taschenatlas Notfall & Rettungsmedizin. Kompendium für den Notarzt, 3rd edn, Berlin.

**Schweitzer, M.; Baumeister, A. (eds.)** (2015), Allgemeine Betriebswirtschaftslehre. Theorie und Politik des Wirtschaftens in Unternehmen, 11. völlig neu bearbeitete Auflage, Berlin.

**Seip, C.; Bill, R.; Kinskofer, A.** (2016), Notfallversorgung der Bevölkerung in Mecklenburg-Vorpommern. In: *Notfall Rettungsmed* 19 (2), pp. 99–107. https://doi.org/10.1007/s10049-015-0117-6.

**Skorning, M.; Bergrath, S.; Brokmann, J. C.; Rörtgen, D.; Beckers, S. K.; Rossaint, R.** (2011), Stellenwert und Potenzial der Telemedizin im Rettungsdienst. In: *Notfall Rettungsmed* 14 (3), pp. 187–191. https://doi.org/10.1007/s10049-010-1397-5.

**Sozialgesetzbuch Fünftes Buch**, Gesetzliche Krankenversicherung, vom 20.12.1988.

**Statistisches Bundesamt** (2022), Gesundheitsausgaben nach Einrichtungen 2018–2020, 22.06.2022. Online verfügbar unter https://www.destatis.de/DE/Themen/Gesellschaft-

Umwelt/Gesundheit/Gesundheitsausgaben/Tabellen/einrichtungen.html, zuletzt geprüft am 22.06.2022.

**Süss, R.; Dewenter, C.; Ekinci, A.; Laslo, T.; Fleßa, S.** (2020), Das Telenotarztsystem – Potentiale für die präklinische Notfallversorgung im ländlichen Raum. In: *Gesundheitsökonomie & Qualitätsmanagement* 25 (03), pp. 163–168. https://doi.org/10.1055/a-1100-2639.

**Süss, R.; Fleßa, S.** (2020), Etablierung einer Telenotarzt-Anwendung. Umsetzungshürden. In: K. Hahnenkamp, S. Fleßa, J. Hasebrook, P. Brinkrolf, B. Metelmann und C. Metelmann (eds.): Notfallversorgung auf dem Land. Ergebnisse des Pilotprojektes Land|Rettung, 1st edn, pp. 136–137, Berlin.

**Weber, J.; Schäffer, U.** (2014), Einführung in das Controlling. 14., überarbeitete und aktualisierte Auflage, Stuttgart.

**Wöhe, G.; Döring, U.** (2013), Einführung in die allgemeine Betriebswirtschaftslehre. 25. überarbeitete und aktualisierte Auflage, München.

**Ziegenfuß, T.** (2021), Notfallmedizin, 8. überarbeitete Auflage, Berlin.

**Zimmermann, H.-J.** (2008), Operations Research. Methoden und Modelle für Wirtschaftsingenieure, Betriebswirte, Informatiker, 2., aktualisierte Auflage, Wiesbaden.

MIX
Papier aus verantwortungsvollen Quellen
Paper from responsible sources
FSC® C105338

If you have any concerns about our products,
you can contact us on
**ProductSafety@springernature.com**

In case Publisher is established outside the EU,
the EU authorized representative is:
**Springer Nature Customer Service Center GmbH**
**Europaplatz 3, 69115 Heidelberg, Germany**

Printed by Libri Plureos GmbH
in Hamburg, Germany